Susan Brookes'
REAL
HOME
COOKING

Susan Brookes'

REAL

HOME

COOKING

HarperCollins*Publishers*

First published in 1998 by HarperCollins*Publishers* in association with The Granada Media Group Limited
Reprinted 1998

A catalogue record for this book is available from the British Library.

ISBN 0 00 414051 6

Colour reproduction in Singapore by Colourscan
Printed and bound in Italy

Cover photograph of Susan Brookes: Will White
Hair and make-up: Jane Hatch
Reportage photographs: Nigel Hillier/UNP
Food photographs: Huw Williams
Stylist: Maureen Kane

For 'This Morning':
Producer/Director: Jason Collier
Home Economists: Claire Bassano, Paul Brodel
    and Anna Swallow
Camera: Geoff Plumb and John Atkins
Sound: Kevin Amos
VT Editor: Chris Clift
Series Editor: Helen Williams

Notes about the recipes

1. Follow either the metric or imperial measurements, rather than mix the two.
2. A glass means a standard wine glass (125 ml/4 fl oz).
3. All eggs are medium (size 3), unless otherwise stated.
4. I use freshly ground black pepper, but ordinary table salt. In the recipes I just say 'salt and pepper'.
5. If I just say 'oil', I have left it for you to choose whichever oil you like to use. Sunflower oil is a good, all-round basic.
6. Spoon measurements are level, unless otherwise stated, and as a guide:

        1 teaspoon = 5 ml
        1 dessertspoon = 10 ml
        1 tablespoon = 15 ml

INTRODUCTION

The recipes in this book are the sort of real home cooking that I make for my family and friends, so if you are looking for restaurant food, save up and go out for a treat. This book is for everyday, family occasions, weekends when friends drop in, days when you are in a hurry or when you fancy being a bit creative in the kitchen – in other words – real life. There are some real British favourites here, so you should find plenty of inspiration to answer the question – what shall I give them tonight?

I feel very lucky to work in food – it has always seemed the best part of This Morning to be in. I don't think I'd be able to deal with people's illnesses or troubles every day, as some of our experts do with such dedication and cheerfulness, year in, year out. At least food is something most people look forward to, and mealtimes are often the highlight of the day. I think it's very important to share a meal and to

spend mealtimes actually talking to each other. The family that eats together, keeps together, doesn't it? I think it has a better chance of it.

Cooking at home is also about knowing exactly what it is you are eating. I think people are beginning to realise that the best chance of knowing what is in the food we eat is to cook it yourself, rather than to rely on ready-made meals. It's a darned sight cheaper, too, and gives you more say in the way of personal preference – seasoning, spiciness, and so on. Good food, freshly cooked and eaten together, is better for us than fast junk food, consumed alone or on the trot between jobs. So even if you don't have time every day, give the recipes in this book a try when you can.

I hope you will enjoy cooking and serving these recipes as much as I have. All of them are straightforward, tried and trusted favourites. I can truly say that my happiest times are spent around the kitchen table, at home. That, for me, is what *Real Home Cooking* is about.

Susan

THE MENUS

The Menus

Menu 17 (page 69)
Donald's Pheasant
Treacle Tart

Menu 18 (page 72)
Sausage and Pâté Plait
Garlic Cabbage
Shirley's Caramel Cream

Menu 19 (page 76)
New Bangers and Mash
Roasted Red Onion Gravy
Autumn Pudding

Menu 20 (page 80)
Roasted Bacon
Old-fashioned Apricot Tart

Menu 21 (page 82)
Gammon with an Orange Mustard Sauce
Cherry Batter Pudding

Menu 22 (page 84)
Pork Ribs with a Spicy Apricot Sauce
Berry Pudding

Menu 23 (page 87)
Pork Collops
Baked Pears in Almond Meringue

Menu 24 (page 90)
Bacon and Beans
Ripon Cheese and Apple Pie

Menu 25 (page 93)
Peppered Beef and Bacon Rolls
Flambéed Fruits
Fudge Sauce

Menu 1

New Kedgeree

Red Salad

Chocolate Orange Roulade

New Kedgeree

serves 4

50 g/2 oz butter or
2 tablespoons vegetable oil

1 onion, chopped

½ teaspoon curry powder

½ teaspoon turmeric

250 g/8 oz long grain rice

¾ pint/450 ml water

2 tins (approximately
200 g/7 oz each) tuna fish in
brine, drained and flaked

1 tin or jar (approximately
200 g/7 oz) stoned black olives

juice of ½ lemon

2 tablespoons
chopped parsley

4 hard-boiled eggs, quartered

salt and pepper

This dish originally came from India, where people would have it for breakfast. Nowadays, we tend to eat less at the start of the day than in those days of groaning Victorian sideboards covered with silver dishes of kedgeree, bacon, ham, eggs, devilled kidneys... it makes my one dish seem quite mean! Kedgeree usually contains smoked haddock, but because this isn't always available, my recipe uses readily-available tinned tuna. You may find it a useful idea to have up your sleeve for when unexpected friends drop in.

1 Heat the butter or oil, then fry the onion until it starts to turn transparent.

2 Add the curry powder and turmeric, stir well, and fry for about 1 minute to release the flavour and colour of the spices.

3 Add the rice and stir well to coat all the grains in the mixture, then pour over the water. Give the rice a good stir, cover with a lid, then bring to the boil. Reduce the heat, and simmer gently for 15 minutes.

4 Nibble a few grains of rice to check whether the rice is done. If you think it needs to cook for a while longer, you may need to add a little more water. If you think the rice is done, and there is too much water left, remove the lid and simmer until all the liquid has been absorbed.

5 Season to taste, then add the tuna, olives, lemon juice, and half the parsley, and gently stir in. Serve garnished with the eggs and the remaining parsley.

Red Salad

serves 4

This light, fresh salad goes well with the New Kedgeree. I often serve cold, sliced vegetable and fruit accompaniments with curried foods, as something cool nicely offsets hot flavours.

1 Mix together the olive oil, red wine vinegar, sugar and a generous seasoning of salt and pepper to make a simple dressing for the salad. I think you get the best result if you shake them together. A screw-top jar, such as a washed-out honey jar, will do the job. If your tomatoes are not very ripe, add a little more sugar to the dressing to balance the acidity.

2 Assemble the salad by placing the lettuce in a large salad bowl, and placing the tomatoes and radishes on top. Pour over the dressing and toss gently.

FOR THE DRESSING:

2 tablespoons olive oil

1 tablespoon red wine vinegar

1 teaspoon sugar

salt and pepper

FOR THE SALAD:

1 red lettuce e.g. radicchio

2 large tomatoes, sliced

1 small bunch radishes, sliced

Chocolate Orange Roulade

serves 6–8

175 g/6 oz plain chocolate, plus extra for decoration (optional)

6 eggs, separated

125 g/4 oz caster sugar, plus extra for dusting

butter or sunflower oil, for greasing

300 ml/½ pint double cream, plus extra for decoration

1 tablespoon brandy or orange liqueur

1 tin (approximately 425 g/ 14 oz) mandarin oranges, drained

1 To make the roulade, break the chocolate into pieces and melt in a bowl over a pan of barely simmering water. Stir until smooth, and remove from the heat.

2 Whisk the egg yolks together, add the sugar, and whisk until pale and foamy.

3 Stir the melted chocolate into this mixture and beat until smooth.

4 Whisk the egg whites in a clean bowl with a clean whisk until stiff (they won't stiffen if there is even the tiniest bit of grease around), then fold gently into the chocolate mixture.

5 Grease a Swiss roll tin (about 20 × 25 cm/8 × 10 inches), and line it with baking parchment. Pour in the roulade mixture and spread it evenly around the tin. Bake in a preheated oven at gas mark 4/180°C/350°F for 20 minutes.

6 Remove the tin from the oven, cover with a damp tea-towel and leave for 10 minutes. Tip the cake out onto a sheet of baking parchment sprinkled with a little caster sugar, and carefully peel off the lining paper. Leave to cool, then trim the cake so you have neat, straight edges.

7 To make the filling, whip the cream and brandy or orange liqueur together until thick and holding its shape.

8 Spread this over the cooled cake, and arrange the mandarin orange pieces (reserve a few for decoration) over the cream fairly evenly, but leaving a gap around the edges.

9 Using the lining paper to help you, roll up the roulade like a Swiss roll. Place on a serving dish or platter with the join underneath.

10 To decorate the roulade, whip some extra double cream and pipe over the top. Decorate with the reserved orange segments. If you are feeling creative, pipe some more melted chocolate onto greaseproof paper to make chocolate leaves, and chill until set.

Menu 2

Crab Cakes

Fresh Tomato Salsa

Burnt Lemon Cream

Crab Cakes

serves 4

250 g/8 oz crabmeat, dark and light mixed

250 g/8 oz mashed, cooked potatoes

2 tablespoons chopped fresh chives

½ teaspoon paprika

1 teaspoon French mustard

3 eggs

flour, for dusting your hands

50 g/2 oz breadcrumbs

50 g/2 oz medium oatmeal

oil, for frying

salt and pepper

I usually make this with tinned crabmeat, as I can't always get fresh, and it always works very well. As there is potato in the cakes, and tomatoes in the salsa accompaniment, you may like to serve these just with fresh bread rolls and a green salad.

1 Put the crabmeat, potatoes, chives, paprika and mustard in a large bowl, and mash together using a fork. Season with salt and pepper to taste.

2 Beat one of the eggs, then gradually add this to the crab mixture. This is to bind the mixture together, so if you find that this isn't quite enough, add some more beaten egg – it will only mean you have a little less for coating.

3 Flour your hands, then shape the crab mixture into 8 round cakes.

4 Beat the remaining 2 eggs, and pour onto a dinner plate. Mix together the breadcrumbs and oatmeal and pour onto another plate.

5 Heat the oil in a large frying pan, then dip each crab cake first in the beaten egg, then in the oatmeal and breadcrumb mixture, to coat on all sides. Place gently in the hot oil and cook for about 5 minutes, turning once. Serve immediately.

Fresh Tomato Salsa

serves 4

Use ripe beef or plum tomatoes if you can get them. This salsa is best if you make it about ½ hour before you want to serve it, so the flavours have time to develop and mingle.

1 Mix all the ingredients together. If you like a chunky consistency you can leave it like this, but for a smoother salsa, whizz it in a food processor. Season with salt and pepper to taste.

750 g/1½ lbs ripe tomatoes, skinned, deseeded and chopped

½ red onion, chopped finely

2 garlic cloves, crushed

1 tablespoon chopped fresh basil

1 red chilli, deseeded and chopped finely

1 tablespoon olive oil

1 tablespoon lemon juice

2 teaspoons sugar

salt and pepper

Burnt Lemon Cream

serves 4

For best results, start this the day before you want to eat it, so it can chill thoroughly overnight. You will have egg whites left over if you make this, so have a look at the Mocha Lemon Curd Meringue recipe on page 64 for a way of using them up.

4 egg yolks

50 g/2 oz caster sugar

300 ml/½ pint double cream

1 teaspoon vanilla extract

grated zest of 1 lemon

4 tablespoons demerara sugar

1 Put the egg yolks and caster sugar into a large bowl, and whisk together until pale and thick – the whisk should leave a trail on the surface when you lift it up.

2 Gently heat the double cream, until just simmering, then remove from the heat.

3 Pour the cream into the egg mixture, whisking all the time, until well mixed. Be sure to take care when you do this as the cream is very hot, and can splatter.

4 Pour the mixture into a clean pan, and heat gently until just simmering again. Stir continuously, using a wooden spoon, gently scraping the mixture from the sides of the pan, until it is thick enough to coat the back of the spoon.

5 Remove from the heat and pour through a sieve into a large jug. Stir in the vanilla extract and lemon zest.

6 Carefully pour the mixture into 4 small, round dishes or ramekins (about 8 cm/3 inches in diameter). Place in the fridge overnight until set.

7 Just before serving, sprinkle over the demerara sugar. Heat your grill to its highest setting, then place the dishes under until the sugar starts to melt into little pools. This will only take a minute, so keep an eye on them. For best results, use a small blow torch. I find that you only need to use about half the amount of sugar, if using a blow torch, and it's much quicker. Start at the side furthest away from you, and wave the blow torch over until the sugar starts to melt. If black specks appear, you are holding it too close. In both cases, when the sugar has melted, leave to cool for about 5 minutes until the top is crisp. Serve immediately.

Menu 3

Plaited Fish

Tomato and Courgette with a Crumb Crust

Sticky Ginger and Apple Puddings

Plaited Fish

serves 2

You need long strips of fish fillet for this recipe, so if you have to buy larger pieces and have some left over, make a fish pie or fishcakes with the trimmings. Once you have prepared the fish, this cooks very quickly, and looks very attractive because of the different colours. It's a favourite with us for a quiet meal in on our own, but it's very easy to multiply this recipe if you want to serve more people.

125 g/4 oz white fish, e.g. whiting or cod

125 g/4 oz yellow fish, e.g. smoked haddock

125 g/4 oz pink fish, e.g. salmon or trout

vegetable oil, for brushing

2 thick slices of lemon

chopped parsley, to decorate

salt and pepper

1 Cut each piece of fish into 2 strips, about 1 cm/½ inch thick and 20 cm/8 inches long.

2 Lay 1 piece of each fish on a piece of foil and plait them together. This will make a shape like a small, plaited bread roll, about 13 cm/5 inches long. Tuck the ends under as neatly as you can, and repeat with the other 3 pieces of fish.

3 Brush a little vegetable oil over the plaits, and season with plenty of salt and pepper. Fold the foil loosely over the fish, and bake in a preheated oven at gas mark 6/200°C/400°F for 10 minutes.

4 Remove from the oven and leave wrapped in the foil for a minute, to firm up the fish. When ready to serve, carefully lift the plaits out of the foil using a fish slice. Spoon over some of the cooking juices. Serve this decorated with the lemon slices half-dipped in some chopped parsley.

Tomato and Courgette with a Crumb Crust

serves 4

This very easy recipe is delicious – the breadcrumb mixture soaks up the wonderful, buttery juices.

50 g/2 oz butter

375 g/12 oz courgettes, sliced thickly

375 g/12 oz ripe tomatoes, sliced thickly

50 g/2 oz brown breadcrumbs

25 g/1 oz Parmesan cheese, grated

salt and pepper

1 Melt the butter in a large frying pan, and add the courgettes. Fry them over a high heat for 5-6 minutes until browned on both sides.

2 Add the tomatoes, stir, and cook for 2 minutes. Season generously with salt and pepper, then tip into an ovenproof gratin dish. I use one which is oval, 28 cm/11 inches by 19 cm/7½ inches.

3 Mix the breadcrumbs and Parmesan cheese together and sprinkle over the top of the tomato and courgette mixture. Place under a hot grill for about 3 minutes, until the top is brown.

Sticky Ginger and Apple Puddings

serves 4

You can buy 'ginger topping', which is just preserved ginger, chopped small. If you use the preserved ginger that comes in large pieces, then you will have a jolly sticky time chopping it up!

1 To make the puddings, first warm together gently in a small pan the ginger topping, butter, sugar and black treacle. Remove from the heat when everything has melted.

2 In a large bowl, mix together the flour, ginger and cinnamon. Make a well in the centre, then pour in the melted ingredients. Fold together, then beat together using a wooden spoon. Add the eggs and mix well.

3 Peel the apple, and grate it directly into the mixture, turning the apple as you grate so that you end up with all the apple but none of the core. Beat well to mix.

4 Put a full kettle on to boil. Meanwhile, divide the pudding mixture between four well-greased, small pudding bowls (about 9 cm/3½ inches in diameter) and stand these in a roasting tin. Pour the boiling water around the bowls so it is about 2.5 cm/1 inch deep. Carefully slide the roasting tin into a preheated oven (gas mark 6/200°C/400°F). Bake for about ½ hour, until the puddings are well-risen and springy.

5 To make the sauce, warm the sauce ingredients together gently in a small pan. When everything is melted and well mixed, serve poured over the Sticky Ginger and Apple Puddings.

FOR THE PUDDINGS:

125 g/4 oz ginger topping

75 g/3 oz butter, plus extra for greasing

125 g/4 oz soft dark brown sugar

1 tablespoon black treacle

175 g/6 oz self-raising flour, preferably wholemeal

1 teaspoon ground ginger

1 teaspoon ground cinnamon

2 eggs, beaten

1 crisp eating apple

FOR THE SAUCE:

125 g/4 oz butter

175 g/6 oz soft brown sugar

1 tablespoon ginger topping

Menu 4

Savoury Cheesecake

Gipsy Banana Tart

Savoury Cheesecake

serves 4–6

I've tried this with different combinations of fish and seafood, but always come back to basic salmon and prawns – sometimes, a classic combination is the best. You can use fresh, or frozen prawns, but if using frozen, defrost and pat dry using kitchen paper before use. It's a useful recipe that can make a light main course for lunch or supper, or thinner slices dressed with some smart salad leaves are a delicious starter. I like to serve this with some crème fraîche with chives snipped into it. The crumb crust makes a nice easy change from pastry.

1 To make the crust, melt the butter and add the breadcrumbs and Parmesan and mix well.

2 Tip the mixture into a greased, round quiche dish (about 20 cm/8 inches in diameter, 4 cm/1½ inches deep). Using your fingers, press the mixture into the base and slightly up the sides of the tin. Don't worry if there isn't enough of it to go all the way up the sides; just cover the base and the angle of the sides. Put this in the fridge to firm up while you make the filling.

3 Heat the oil in a small frying pan, and fry the onion and pepper for about 5 minutes, until they start to soften.

4 Whisk the eggs, cream and cream cheese together in a bowl until smooth and starting to thicken. Mix with the onion and pepper mixture.

5 Stir in the Parmesan and paprika or Cajun seasoning, and season to taste with salt.

6 Add the prawns and salmon and mix well. Pour over the crumb crust.

7 Bake in a preheated oven at gas mark 4/180°C/350°F for about 1 hour, by which time the filling should be starting to go golden brown on top and nearly set – it will firm up as it cools. Serve just warm (though it is good cold, too).

FOR THE CRUST:

50 g/2 oz butter, plus extra for greasing

50 g/2 oz fresh breadcrumbs

25 g/1 oz Parmesan cheese, grated

FOR THE FILLING:

1 tablespoon oil, for frying

8 spring onions, sliced

¼ red or yellow pepper, deseeded and diced

2 large eggs

2 tablespoons double cream

175 g/6 oz cream cheese

25 g/1 oz Parmesan cheese, grated

½ teaspoon paprika or Cajun seasoning

125 g/4 oz prawns

275 g/9 oz salmon fillet, skinned and cut into 1 cm/½ inch pieces

salt

Gipsy Banana Tart

serves 4–6

This is like Banoffee pie, but is much quicker and easier to make. Use raw cane light muscovado sugar – it will say this on the packet – to be sure of getting a good set. This is good served with double cream, but for a change, try serving it with banana-flavour yoghurt.

1 Roll out the pastry on a floured surface, and use to line a greased, round, loose-bottomed flan dish (about 20-22 cm/8-8½ inches in diameter).

2 Slice 3 of the peeled bananas over the pastry and arrange in an even layer over the base. Mix the sugar and condensed milk together in a bowl, then pour over the banana slices.

3 Bake in a preheated oven at gas mark 4/180°C/350°F for 20 minutes, by which time the filling should be about set – it will firm up further as it cools.

4 You can serve this just warm, when it has cooled a little, or serve it cold. Slice the remaining banana and use to decorate the tart.

250 g/8 oz shortcrust pastry

flour, for dusting

butter, for greasing

4 bananas

175 g/6 oz raw cane light muscovado sugar

425 g/14 oz sweetened condensed milk

29

Menu 5

Winter Vegetable Bake

Rhubarb and Orange Dessert

Winter Vegetable Bake

serves 4

500 g/1 lb carrots, sliced

1 medium leek, sliced

375 g/12 oz Savoy cabbage (discard the outer leaves)

300 ml/½ pint milk

50 g/2 oz butter, cut into pieces, plus extra for greasing

50 g/2 oz white plain flour

1 teaspoon French mustard

175 g/6 oz mature Cheddar cheese, grated

75 g/3 oz chopped toasted hazelnuts

salt and pepper

1 Cook the carrots in lightly salted, boiling water for 10 minutes.

2 Add the leek and simmer for a further 3-4 minutes, then drain in a colander or sieve.

3 Cut the cabbage into quarters and discard the stalk. Slice, and boil in a fresh pan of lightly salted, boiling water for just 2 minutes. Drain the cabbage and refresh under running cold water. This stops the cabbage overcooking, and helps to keep the colour.

4 Make a white sauce by pouring the milk into a pan and adding the butter and flour, all at once. Whisk over a gentle heat and bring to the boil. Reduce the heat until the sauce is simmering and cook gently for 1 minute, until the sauce is thick. Remove from the heat.

5 Add the mustard and most of the cheese to the sauce, and stir until melted. Season with salt and pepper to taste.

6 Grease an ovenproof dish. I make this in a square ovenproof dish that has sides of 24 cm/9½ inches, and is 5 cm/2 inches deep. Place half the cabbage in the bottom of the dish, and cover with about half of the leek and carrot mixture.

7 Spread just under half the sauce over the vegetables, as evenly as you can, then sprinkle over half the nuts. Layer the remaining cabbage on top, followed by the remaining carrot and leek mixture.

8 Spread the rest of the sauce over, then sprinkle on the remaining nuts and cheese.

9 Bake in a preheated oven at gas mark 6/200°C/400°F for about 15 minutes, until golden brown and bubbling.

Rhubarb and Orange Dessert

serves 2–3

250 g/8 oz trimmed rhubarb, cut into 2 cm/1 inch chunks

grated zest and juice of 1 large orange

2 tablespoons caster sugar

200 g/7 oz thick Greek yoghurt

a few toasted flaked almonds and sprigs of mint, for decoration (optional)

1 Place the rhubarb in a pan with the grated orange zest, about 2 tablespoons of the juice and the sugar. Bring to the boil, then reduce the heat and simmer without a lid for about 10 minutes until the rhubarb is soft. Stir from time to time.

2 Remove the pan from the heat, allow the rhubarb to cool a little, and then purée it in a blender or food processor. Chill in the fridge.

3 When you are ready to assemble the dessert, put a spoonful of the rhubarb mixture in the bottom of 2 or 3 stemmed serving glasses, then add a spoonful of the yoghurt. Continue like this, alternately, until all used up, ending with a spoonful of rhubarb. Serve chilled, garnished with a generous sprinkle of flaked almonds and a sprig of mint, if using.

Menu 6

Salmon Fishcakes

Lemon Parsley Sauce

Chocolate and Almond Trifle

Salmon Fishcakes

serves 4

The salmon and the mashed potato need to be cold, so this is a good way of using up leftovers. You can always add some tinned salmon if you don't have enough. These are very nice served with lightly cooked sugar snap or mangetout peas.

375 g/12 oz cooked salmon fillet, flaked, skin and bones removed

375 g/12 oz mashed, cooked potatoes

2 hard-boiled eggs, peeled and chopped

½ teaspoon paprika

2 tablespoons chopped chives

2 tablespoons mayonnaise

flour, for dusting

vegetable oil, for frying

125 g/4 oz fresh brown breadcrumbs

1 egg, beaten

salt

1 Put the salmon, potato, eggs, paprika, chives and mayonnaise in a large bowl and mash together with a fork. Season to taste with salt.

2 Flour your hands, then shape the mixture into 8 cakes.

3 To cook the fishcakes, heat the oil in a large frying pan, spread the breadcrumbs out on a dinner plate, and pour the beaten egg onto another plate next to it. Dip each fishcake in the beaten egg, then in the breadcrumbs, to coat on both sides. Fry the cakes in the hot oil for 3-4 minutes on each side, until they are golden brown, and drain well before serving. Serve 2 fishcakes per person with the Lemon Parsley Sauce poured over.

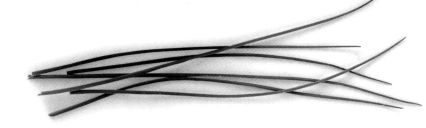

Lemon Parsley Sauce

makes 300 ml/½ pint

1 Pour the milk into a pan, and bring to a simmer over a medium heat. Add the flour, all at once, and whisk, using a small balloon whisk, until well mixed.

2 Add the butter little by little, while you continue to whisk, adding butter as it melts. The sauce will thicken as it comes up to the boil, and you should then add the parsley. Cook for a further minute.

3 Remove the sauce from the heat, add the lemon juice, and season to taste. Serve immediately.

300 ml/½ pint milk

1 tablespoon white plain flour

1 tablespoon butter

2 tablespoons chopped parsley

1 tablespoon lemon juice

salt and pepper

Chocolate and Almond Trifle

serves 6

I like to decorate this using extra double cream, small ratafia biscuits (which continue the almond flavour) and crystallised violets.

1 Arrange the Swiss roll slices around the base and sides of a glass bowl, and tuck the pieces of orange between the gaps.

2 Pour 4 tablespoons of the Amaretto liqueur over the Swiss roll.

3 Break the chocolate into a bowl placed over a pan of barely simmering hot water, and mix together with the coffee until smooth. Remove from the heat, and leave to cool for 2-3 minutes.

4 Add the remaining liqueur and the egg yolks, and beat together.

5 Whisk the cream until it is thick and floppy and just holding its shape. In another bowl, whisk the egg whites until they form stiff peaks.

6 Fold the cream into the chocolate mixture, then fold in the stiff egg whites. Pour this into the bowl containing the Swiss roll, and chill for at least 1 hour before serving.

1 small chocolate Swiss roll, sliced thinly

2 oranges, or 1 tin (approximately 425 g/14 oz) mandarin segments, cut into small pieces

6 tablespoons Amaretto (almond) liqueur

125 g/4 oz dark chocolate

1 tablespoon strong black coffee

3 eggs, separated

150 ml/¼ pint double cream

Menu
7
Easter Menu

Menu
7

Easter Pie

Lemon-buttered Corn and Carrots

Simnel Cake

Easter Pie

serves 4–6

I first heard about this recipe from a North Italian friend who is a great home cook. In Italy it is called Torta Pascalina, *which roughly translates to 'Easter Pie'. The use of golden and green ingredients is meant to symbolise springtime. The pastry is always puff or flaky pastry, and it was originally supposed to have 33 layers, to symbolise the number of years Jesus lived before he died at the first Easter. It is a good recipe to serve for those who don't eat meat.*

1 Heat the butter or oil in a large frying pan, and gently fry the garlic and chives, until the garlic starts to soften.

2 Add the spinach and cook for a further 5 minutes, stirring often, then remove from the heat. Season with salt and pepper to taste, and leave to cool.

3 In a small bowl, beat one of the eggs with a fork, then, leaving just a little in the bowl to use for brushing over the pie plate, beat the rest into the cream cheese.

4 Add the nutmeg and Parmesan cheese, and stir until well mixed. When the spinach mixture is cooled, mix the two together.

5 Lightly grease a round pie dish (about 20 cm/8 inches in diameter, 5 cm/2 inches deep). Divide the puff pastry in half, and roll out one half on a well-floured surface, until large enough to line the pie dish.

6 Spread the cheese and spinach filling over this, and use a dessertspoon to make three indentations in the filling, large enough to take the remaining eggs. Break 1 egg into each hole.

7 Roll out the remaining pastry until large enough to make a lid. Brush water around the edge of the pie, then place the lid over the top. Brush the pie with the reserved beaten egg, then bake in a preheated oven at gas mark 6/200°C/400°F for 30-40 minutes, until golden brown. This is best eaten warm, but it can be served cold.

25 g/1 oz butter or olive oil, plus extra for greasing

1 garlic clove, crushed

1 tablespoon chopped fresh chives

250 g/8 oz chopped frozen spinach

4 eggs

250 g/8 oz cream cheese

¼ teaspoon grated nutmeg

75 g/3 oz Parmesan cheese, grated

400 g/13 oz puff pastry

flour, for dusting

salt and pepper

Lemon-buttered Corn and Carrots

serves 4

500 g/1 lb carrots, peeled and cut into sticks approximately 3.5 cm/1½ inches long

grated zest and juice of ½ lemon

a small knob of butter

125 g/4 oz drained sweetcorn (tinned or frozen)

salt

1 Place the carrots in a large saucepan with the lemon zest and juice and pour over just enough water to cover. Bring to the boil, and simmer gently, without a lid, for about 20 minutes until the carrots are cooked and most of the water has evaporated. Watch that the carrots don't boil dry and shake the pan from time to time so the carrots cook evenly.

2 Add the butter and the sweetcorn and heat through, stirring gently until most of the liquid has evaporated, leaving just a little buttery juice. Add salt to taste.

Simnel Cake

serves 11

This traditional rich fruit cake is made with 11 balls of marzipan on top, to commemorate all the apostles except for Judas. If primroses are in flower, they make a nice decoration.

1 Cream the butter and sugar together until light and fluffy.

2 In a large mixing bowl, mix together the wholemeal flour, self-raising flour, nutmeg, dried fruit and nuts.

3 Add alternate spoonfuls of the beaten egg and the flour mixture to the creamed mixture until all used up, mixing well between each addition.

4 Spoon half the mixture into a lightly-greased and lined, round, deep cake tin (about 20 cm/8 inches in diameter), and smooth until the mixture is level.

5 Roll out one of the blocks of marzipan on a surface lightly dusted with icing sugar, to make a circle slightly smaller than the cake tin. Place the circle on top of the mixture. Spread the remaining cake mixture over the marzipan circle, and smooth until level.

6 Bake the cake for 2 hours in a preheated oven at gas mark 3/160°C/325°F. Leave to cool in the tin.

7 When ready to finish the cake, roll out one of the remaining blocks of marzipan to make a circle that will just cover the surface of the cake. Brush the warmed jam or honey over the top of the cake – this will help the marzipan stick to the cake. Turn the cake upside down, and place it centrally over the marzipan circle. Trim the edges, then turn the cake upright.

8 Use the remaining block of marzipan to make 11 small balls, each about the size of a small walnut. Make 11 indentations around the top edge of the cake, and drizzle a little more warmed jam or honey into each hole. Place a ball in each hole.

9 For a nice finishing touch, brown the surface of the cake under a preheated grill for just a few seconds. Don't take your eyes off it, as it will brown very quickly.

250 g/8 oz butter, softened, plus extra for greasing

250 g/8 oz soft brown sugar

175 g/6 oz wholemeal plain flour

175 g/6 oz white self-raising flour

½ teaspoon grated nutmeg

500 g/1 lb mixed dried fruit

125 g/4 oz chopped walnuts or hazelnuts

4 eggs, beaten

3 × 250 g/8 oz blocks of marzipan

icing sugar, for dusting

a little apricot jam or honey, warmed

Menu 8

Skipton Pie

Baked Stuffed Nectarines

Butterscotch Sauce

Skipton Pie

serves 4

1 tablespoon oil

1 onion, chopped

500 g/1 lb minced lamb

125 g/4 oz mushrooms, chopped

300 ml/½ pint vegetable stock

a dash of mushroom ketchup or Worcestershire sauce

1 kg/2 lbs potatoes, cut into chunks

a little milk and butter, for mashing

2 tablespoons chopped fresh parsley

salt and pepper

This pie is named after the market town near where I live, which originally meant sheep town. It is still the centre of a sheep farming area, set amongst beautiful countryside where you can pick wild mushrooms for free – so long as you know where to look and are on good terms with the local farmer.

1 Heat the oil in a large pan, and fry the onion until it starts to brown.

2 Add the lamb, and fry all over until browned, then stir in the chopped mushrooms.

3 Add the stock, mushroom ketchup or Worcestershire sauce, mix well, and season to taste (take care when adding salt if you have used a salty stock cube). Simmer, stirring occasionally, for half an hour.

4 Boil the potatoes in lightly salted water for about 20 minutes. Drain, add a small knob of butter and a little milk, and mash until smooth. I find I get the best results by starting with a potato masher, then finishing by beating well with a fork. Mix in a little seasoning and the chopped parsley.

5 Spoon the cooked meat mixture into the base of a round, ovenproof dish (about 20 cm/8 inches in diameter). Make sure that any juices do not come up higher than the surface of the meat – this is so the topping sits on top.

6 Spoon the mashed potato over the meat mixture, then use a fork to make a covering. I like quite a rough pattern on the surface – there is no need to smooth it over. Place under a hot grill for a few minutes until brown and crispy.

Note
This will keep happily in a very low oven for an hour or two, so is an ideal dish to make before going out, as it will be ready to serve as soon as you get back.

Baked Stuffed Nectarines

serves 1

This recipe is easy to adapt for any number of people, so I have given the amounts needed for one, so you can make as many as you like.

1 tablespoon cream cheese

½ tablespoon caster sugar

½ tablespoon ground almonds

1 nectarine, halved and stoned

a few flaked almonds, for decoration

1 Place the cream cheese and sugar in a bowl, and beat together until smooth. This is easiest if you remove the cheese from the fridge before you want to use it, so it has time to soften.

2 Work the ground almonds into the cheese mixture to form a fairly stiff paste, and pile this mixture into each half of the fruit, pressing down into the cavity left by the stone.

3 Arrange the stuffed nectarine halves in an ovenproof dish, and place a few flaked almonds on top of each.

4 Bake in a preheated oven at gas mark 6/200°C/400°F for about 8 minutes, until the fruit is hot and the almonds toasted.

5 You can serve this as it is or with thick plain yoghurt, or go for broke and serve it with Butterscotch Sauce.

Butterscotch Sauce

serves 6

My daughter says you might just as well slap the calories straight onto your thighs as eat this – but I haven't noticed her refuse to eat it yet! This can be served hot or cold, and will keep for a week if kept in a jar in the fridge.

50 g/2 oz butter

75 g/3 oz soft dark brown sugar

50 g/2 oz granulated sugar

150 g/5 oz golden syrup

125 ml/4 fl oz double cream

½ teaspoon vanilla extract

1 Warm the butter, brown sugar, granulated sugar and golden syrup together in a small pan, over a gentle heat, until melted together and smooth.

2 Stir in the cream and vanilla extract, and stir until well mixed and warmed through.

Menu 9

Lamb's Liver in Thyme
  with an Orange and Onion Gravy

Turnover Pear and Cinnamon Pudding

Lamb's Liver in Thyme with an Orange and Onion Gravy

serves 2

I like to make this using onion marmalade, but if you don't have any, you can use sliced red onion. I've explained how to make it both ways. I serve this with new or mashed potatoes and a green vegetable.

1 tablespoon white plain flour

1 tablespoon chopped fresh thyme

50 g/2 oz butter

275 g/9 oz sliced lamb's liver

2 tablespoons red wine

2 tablespoons orange juice

1 tablespoon onion marmalade or ½ red onion, sliced

salt and pepper

1 Spread the flour on a dinner plate, and sprinkle lots of pepper and the thyme over the surface.

2 Heat the butter in a large frying pan, and while it is warming, coat both sides of each slice of liver in the seasoned flour. Lay the liver in the butter and fry gently for 2 minutes on each side. The liver will still be a little pink in the middle, but will continue to cook a bit more as you keep it warm, so only give it another ½ minute on one side if you're really sure you want it cooked for longer.

3 Remove the liver and keep warm on a serving dish while you make the gravy. At this stage, if you are using fresh red onion, add the onion to the pan juices and fry for a few minutes until soft.

4 Pour the red wine into the pan juices and stir and scrape to deglaze the pan. Add the orange juice and bubble over a high heat for a couple of minutes to reduce and concentrate the flavour. Add the spoonful of onion marmalade if you haven't used sliced onion.

5 Add salt to taste and heat through. Serve poured over the liver.

46

Turnover Pear and Cinnamon Pudding

serves 4–6

1 Generously grease the base and sides of a round cake tin (about 20 cm/8 inches in diameter). When I say 'generously', I mean it – you should be able to see the yellow of the butter showing in some places!

2 Mix the sugar and cinnamon together, and sprinkle inside the tin.

3 Peel the pears, halve them, and remove the cores. Slice each half lengthways into about three, then arrange the pear slices over the sugar in a sunburst pattern, with the small end of the slices pointing towards the centre.

4 Next, make the pastry. To make it by hand, sieve together a pinch of salt, the sugar and flour, then rub in the butter until the mixture resembles fine breadcrumbs. Add the egg, and mix until you have a soft dough. To make using a food processor, add the ingredients in this order, through the funnel, with the processor running continuously.

5 Roll, or pat out the pastry on a floured surface to make a lid. Make the circle a little larger than the diameter of the tin, and when you place the lid over, tuck in the edges.

6 Bake in a preheated oven at gas mark 6/200°C/400°F for 20-30 minutes, until the pastry is crisp and brown.

7 Leave to cool in the tin for 5 minutes or so before running a knife round the edge to loosen it. Then put a large plate over the top and turn the tin over. Give it a good shake to turn the pudding out. The pears should face upwards when you lift off the tin. You can serve this hot or cold.

butter, for greasing

50 g/2 oz soft brown sugar

1 teaspoon ground cinnamon

3 firm, ripe pears

FOR THE PASTRY:

a pinch of salt

25 g/1 oz caster sugar

300 g/10 oz white self-raising flour, plus extra for dusting

175 g/6 oz butter

1 large egg, beaten

Note
Don't try to make this in a loose-bottomed tin, or all the juice will leak out.

Menu 10

Devilled Lamb Chops

Apple and Blackberry Brown Betty

Devilled Lamb Chops

serves 4

I serve this with garden peas and new potatoes that have been tossed in butter and garnished with chopped fresh mint.

4 sprigs of rosemary

4 garlic cloves, crushed

4 teaspoons mild French mustard

4 large lamb chops or 8 cutlets

1 Pick the rosemary leaves off the stalk, and chop finely – you will have to do this by hand as it will clog up the blades of a food processor.

2 Mix the chopped rosemary with the garlic and mustard to make a paste. Spread this on both sides of the chops or cutlets.

3 Place the chops or cutlets on a rack inside a roasting tin and roast in a preheated oven at gas mark 6/200°C/400°F until cooked to your liking. Fifteen minutes will be enough if you like lamb quite pink, 20 minutes for well done.

Apple and Blackberry Brown Betty

serves 4

I always make this in the autumn, when I can gather the blackberries for free from the hedgerows. If you can't get your hands on blackberries, it works very well with just the simple tang of apples. Just increase the quantity.

1 Peel and core the apples, and slice them into a bowl containing the lemon juice, turning the slices to coat in the juice to prevent them turning brown.

2 Rinse the blackberries and add to the apple slices. Add the apricot jam and mix together.

3 Put the oats, flour, sugar, cinnamon, salt and 75 g/ 3 oz of the butter into another bowl, and rub in with your fingers, until you have a mixture that resembles breadcrumbs.

4 Grease an oval, ovenproof dish (about 28 cm/11 inches in length), and spread half the apple mixture over the base. Spread half the flour and oat mixture over this, then spread over the remaining apple mixture. Finish with a layer of flour and oats. Dot over the remaining butter.

5 Bake in a preheated oven at gas mark 5/190°C/375°F for ¾-1 hour, until the apples are tender and the topping is crisp and golden brown.

500 g/1 lb cooking apples

1 tablespoon lemon juice

250 g/8 oz blackberries

2 tablespoons apricot jam

75 g/3 oz rolled oats

75 g/3 oz wholemeal plain flour

125 g/4 oz soft brown sugar

1 teaspoon ground cinnamon

a pinch of salt

125 g/4 oz butter, plus extra for greasing

Menu 11

Lemon and Coconut Chicken

Chocolate Pie in a Nut Crust

Lemon and Coconut Chicken

serves 2

After filming in Thailand some years ago, I wanted to try cooking some of the dishes myself, but couldn't always get the right ingredients back home. Now it's much easier to get fresh coriander, lemon grass and coconut milk, but it does depend on where you live. This is good served with boiled rice sprinkled with more chopped coriander.

1 tablespoon vegetable oil

2 chicken breasts, skinned

2 tablespoons lemon juice

3 tablespoons water

50 g/2 oz block of creamed coconut

1 tablespoon desiccated coconut

1 tablespoon chopped fresh coriander

salt and pepper

1 Heat the oil in a large frying pan (use a pan with a lid), and fry the chicken until browned on both sides.

2 Add the lemon juice and water, put the lid on, and simmer for about 10 minutes, until the chicken is cooked through. Test by sticking a knife into the thickest part of the meat, then squeezing some juice out. If the juice runs clear, the meat is cooked; if the juices are red in colour, then you will need to cook the chicken for a little longer.

3 Remove the chicken pieces and keep warm. Simmer the juices left in the pan over a gentle heat, and add the creamed coconut, cutting it into chunks in the pan as it starts to melt, and stirring until melted and well mixed.

4 Season to taste, then pour over the chicken pieces. Keep in a warm place.

5 Toast the coconut under a hot grill until dark brown. This not only looks more appetising, but also brings out the flavour of the coconut. Sprinkle the coconut and the chopped fresh coriander over the chicken just before serving.

Chocolate Pie in a Nut Crust

serves 6

I prefer pecan nuts for this recipe, as it is an American pie, but if you can't get them, or don't like them, use walnuts or hazelnuts – they will work just as well. I decorate this with a lattice of piped cream, and put bits of deep purple crystallised violets at the intersections.

FOR THE NUT CRUST:

125 g /4 oz butter

125 g /4 oz pecan nuts, finely chopped

125 g /4 oz brown breadcrumbs

75 g /3 oz soft brown sugar

FOR THE FILLING:

1 tablespoon cornflour

2 tablespoons water

1 tablespoon orange juice

125 g/4 oz dark chocolate

300 ml/½ pint milk

double cream and crystallised violets, for decoration (optional)

1 To make the nut crust, first melt the butter, then, using a wooden spoon, mix in the nuts, breadcrumbs and sugar.

2 Press this mixture into the base and sides of a well-greased, round pie dish (about 23 cm/9 inches in diameter). Smooth all round using a spatula or the back of a wooden spoon, then shape the edge by pinching with finger and thumb to make a wavy edge.

3 Bake the crust in a preheated oven at gas mark 4/180°C/350°F for about 15 minutes. The crust might bubble up a little during baking, but if this happens, smooth it down again with the back of a metal spoon when you take it out of the oven. Leave to cool while you make the filling.

4 Mix the cornflour with the water and orange juice until smooth.

5 Break the chocolate into pieces and put in a pan with the milk. Melt the chocolate over a low heat, stirring from time to time, until the chocolate has melted, and has blended with the milk.

6 Remove the pan from the heat, and stir in the cornflour mixture.

7 Still stirring, return the pan to the heat and bring to the boil, and stir until thickened and smooth. Pour the mixture into the nut crust. Cover the pie with clingfilm to prevent a skin forming, and leave to cool.

8 If you like, pipe double cream over the surface in a lattice pattern, and decorate with crystallised violets.

Menu 12

Coronation Street Chicken

Rum and Coconut Ice Cream

Coronation Street Chicken

serves 4–6

The inspiration for this recipe was the famous Coronation chicken made for the Queen's coronation lunch in 1952. I've altered it a bit to take in more fruit, and to cater for lighter appetites by using yoghurt as well as mayonnaise. As it is tasty, reliable, and good value, it's a recipe that is always popular. What better, then, than to name it after the nation's favourite Soap! I serve this on a bed of lettuce, with chunks of garlic bread.

1 × 1.5 kg/3½ lb cooked chicken

125 g /4 oz seedless green grapes

300 ml/½ pint mayonnaise

300 ml/½ pint natural yoghurt

2-4 teaspoons curry powder, according to taste

125 g /4 oz celery, sliced thinly

50 g/2 oz no-soak dried apricots, quartered

1 Take the chicken meat off the bones, discard any skin and gristle, and cut the meat into bite-sized pieces.

2 Take the grapes off the stalk and rinse them thoroughly.

3 In a large bowl, mix together the mayonnaise, yoghurt, and curry powder, then add the chicken, celery, grapes and apricots. Mix well until all the dry ingredients are fully coated in the mayonnaise mixture.

Rum and Coconut Ice Cream

serves 2

For this recipe, you need a lot of large bowls. I know this because the first time my husband made it, the amount of washing-up beggared belief. It is worth it though, and my only advice is: don't be tempted to add extra rum – alcohol freezes at a different temperature to water, and too much rum could mean your ice cream doesn't set. If you have any desiccated coconut in the cupboard, toast it, and sprinkle over the ice cream for a crunchy topping.

200 g/7 oz block of creamed coconut, grated

200 ml/7 fl oz coconut milk

1 tablespoon caster sugar

2 eggs, separated

1 tablespoon clear honey

450 ml/¾ pint double cream

2 tablespoons rum

1 Mix together the creamed coconut, coconut milk and caster sugar.

2 In another bowl, beat the egg yolks together with the honey.

3 In yet another bowl, whisk the eggs whites until they are stiff.

4 You're not going to believe this, but in bowl number 4, whisk the cream until it is thick and just holds its shape.

5 Fold the cream into the egg yolk and honey mixture, mix well, then fold in the stiff egg whites.

6 Fold in the coconut mixture and rum, then transfer to a suitable container. This makes about 1 litre/1¾ pints, so an old ice cream container with a lid is ideal.

7 Freeze for several hours, preferably overnight. It needs to be taken out of the freezer about 15 minutes before you want to eat it, so that it softens enough to serve. This will keep well in the freezer for at least 1 month.

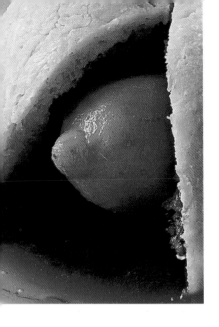

Menu 13

Oven-fried Chicken

Corn Fritters

Lemon Pond Pudding

Oven-fried Chicken

serves 4

This recipe was given to me by an American airman living in Norfolk. He had a young family and didn't think deep-fat fryers and little children were a good combination, so he adapted his 'mom's' method and fried it in the oven instead, which is safer, less fatty, and gives a good, crisp result. This is traditionally served with sweetcorn, on or off the cob, or (my choice) Corn Fritters.

2 eggs

½ teaspoon salt

2 teaspoons Cajun seasoning (or a mixture of paprika and dried mixed herbs)

1 tablespoon lemon juice

125 g/4 oz breadcrumbs

8 small chicken joints (skinned and boned thighs are best)

50 g/2 oz white plain flour

50 g/2 oz butter, melted

1 Beat the eggs together with the salt, Cajun seasoning and lemon juice. Spread the breadcrumbs out on a plate.

2 Coat each piece of chicken in the flour. (An easy way to do this is to put the flour and chicken in a bag and shake it to coat.) Dip the chicken pieces in the beaten egg mixture to coat, then in the breadcrumbs, and place on a roasting tray.

3 Pour the melted butter carefully over the chicken pieces, and bake in a preheated oven at gas mark 6/200°C/400°F for 30 minutes, turning once during the cooking time.

Corn Fritters

makes about 12

1 Whisk the eggs and milk together, then whisk in the salt and flour. When you have a thick batter with bubbles appearing on the surface, stir in the sweetcorn.

2 Heat the oil in a large frying pan until hot. It should be hot enough to crisp a drop of batter when you drop it in.

3 Pour in a tablespoon of batter at a time (my pan will take three fritters at once), and fry for about 45 seconds-1 minute on the first side. It is done when the fritter looks dry at the edges with bubbles forming. Flip over and cook for a little less time on the second side, until golden brown and crisp. Drain well on kitchen paper before serving. Repeat until all the batter is used.

2 eggs

300 ml/½ pint milk

½ teaspoon salt

250 g/8 oz white self-raising flour

1 tin (approximately 325 g/ 11 oz) sweetcorn, drained

2 tablespoons vegetable oil

Lemon Pond Pudding

serves 6

I first heard about this pudding from a director I was working with, who said his wife made it from an old family recipe. I thought the method sounded a bit unlikely, but I can remember jotting down the recipe while we were travelling somewhere in the back of a minibus. I didn't find my notes until later, when, fortunately, I had time to give it a try. After a few experiments with the steaming time, I found it was the most luscious, rich – yet sharp – steamed pudding I had ever tasted. I've since found a similar recipe which seems to come from Sussex, so thanks, Mike and Sussex – it works a treat! This is best steamed but it can be cooked in a microwave. Believe it or not, the lemon will be soft enough to eat – peel and all.

175 g/6 oz white self-raising flour, plus extra for dusting

¼ teaspoon salt

75 g/3 oz vegetarian suet

cold water, to mix

1 large lemon

75 g/3 oz butter, cut into small pieces, plus extra for greasing

75 g/3 oz soft brown sugar

Note
8 minutes is about right for an average, 700 watt microwave oven. If your oven is substantially more powerful than this, cook for 7 minutes. If less powerful, cook for 10 minutes.

1 Put the flour, salt and suet in a bowl and mix together. Add just enough cold water to make a soft dough, but without it getting sticky – 125 ml/4 fl oz is about right.

2 Knead the dough lightly on a well-floured surface with floured hands. Roll out ¾ of the dough, and use it to line the base and sides of a greased 1 litre/1¾ pint pudding basin.

3 Wash the lemon (sometimes they are waxed to preserve the skin, so it might need a good scrub) and prick all over with a skewer.

4 Put a few pieces of the butter and a spoonful of the sugar in the bottom of the lined basin, and add the lemon. Fill up the sides of the basin around and over the lemon with the rest of the sugar and butter.

5 Roll out the remaining dough to make a lid. Moisten the edges of the pudding with a little water, and press the lid into place, tucking in any overlapping edges.

6 If you are going to steam the pudding, cover the basin with a piece of foil that has been pleated to allow for the pudding to rise a little, and tie in place. Put a trivet or upturned saucer in the bottom of a large pan, and put the basin on top. Pour around boiling water to come halfway up the basin. Put a lid on the pan, bring the water to the boil. Turn down the heat and simmer, topping up the water as necessary, for 2½ hours. To microwave, cover the top of the basin loosely with clingfilm, and microwave on high for 8 minutes.

7 Leave the pudding to stand for 10 mintes before serving. To turn the pudding out, run a knife around the edge of the bowl. Place a plate on top of the pudding, and carefully turn it out onto a warmed plate.

Menu 14

Macaroni Bake

Snow Queen of Puddings

Macaroni Bake

serves 4–6

This is a great way of using up leftover chicken or turkey, but it is delicious enough to try for its own sake – it's the sort of family food that is popular with everyone.

250 g/8 oz macaroni

75 g/3 oz butter, cut into small pieces, plus extra for coating the macaroni

900 ml/1½ pints milk

75 g /3 oz white plain flour

250 g/8 oz mature Cheddar cheese, grated

250 g/8 oz cooked turkey or chicken, cut into bite-sized chunks

4 medium tomatoes, sliced

salt and pepper

1 Cook the macaroni in boiling, lightly salted water. The cooking time will depend on the size of the macaroni, so check on the packet. The sort I use is small, and takes just 3 minutes. Drain the macaroni and rinse it under cold water. Toss in a little butter – this stops the macaroni from sticking together, and also adds flavour.

2 Heat the milk in a pan until simmering gently, then add the flour in one go, whisking continuously. Add the butter gradually, continuing to whisk. When the sauce comes up to the boil and begins to thicken, simmer for a further 30 seconds to cook the flour through, then season and remove from the heat.

3 Add 175 g/6 oz of the cheese. Stir the sauce until the cheese has melted, then fold in the cooked macaroni.

4 Layer a large ovenproof dish with about half the macaroni mixture. Place the turkey or chicken and the tomato slices over this. Season with salt and lots of pepper. Spoon the rest of the macaroni mixture over the top, then sprinkle over the remaining cheese.

5 Bake in a preheated oven at gas mark 4/180°C/350°F for about 30 minutes. The top should be golden brown by then, but if you like it crisper, pop it under a hot grill for 2 minutes, just before serving.

Snow Queen of Puddings

serves 4–6

This is a traditional pudding, useful for making when you have very little in the larder. It always reminds me of the most severe winter I can remember (just!), in 1947. The snow in our back yard was higher than me, and getting provisions was a tough business. They had to be dragged home on a sledge, on roads you could hardly see because the snow had drifted higher than the stone walls.

1 Heat the butter and milk together in a pan until the butter has melted and the milk is lukewarm.

2 Mix the breadcrumbs, lemon juice, and a spoonful of the sugar together in a large bowl, then pour the milk mixture over. Leave to stand for 3 minutes, then beat the egg yolks in.

3 Pour the mixture into a greased, ovenproof dish (about 25 cm/10 inches square) and bake in a preheated oven at gas mark 4/180°C/350°F for 30 minutes, by which time it should be just set. Take the pudding out to cool a little, but leave the oven on.

4 Make the meringue mixture by whisking the egg whites until very stiff, then gradually whisking in the remaining sugar until firm and glossy.

5 Warm the jam to make it easier to spread, and carefully smooth it over the surface of the baked pudding. Spread the meringue mix over the jam, taking it right to the edges of the dish. Place back in the oven for about 10 minutes until the surface of the meringue is golden and crisp. Serve immediately.

50 g/2 oz butter, plus extra for greasing

600 ml/1 pint milk

150 g/5 oz breadcrumbs

a dash of lemon juice

150 g/5 oz caster sugar

6 eggs, separated

4 tablespoons red jam (any flavour)

Menu 15

Duck with a Rhubarb and Ginger Sauce
Mocha Lemon Curd Meringue

Duck with a Rhubarb and Ginger Sauce

serves 2

This a favourite with my elder daughter, and is the nearest she gets to eating red meat. The salt should make the skin on the duck nice and crisp, as salt draws out moisture. Try it with Garlic Cabbage (see page 73), or some noodles.

2 duck breasts

1 heaped teaspoon salt

125 g/4 oz rhubarb, cut into 2 cm/1 inch chunks

1 tablespoon water

1 tablespoon sugar

1 teaspoon minced fresh ginger

pepper

1 Place the duck breasts in a roasting tin, skin side up, and sprinkle the salt over the skin.

2 Roast in a preheated oven at gas mark 6/200°C/400°F for 10 minutes, then turn down to gas mark 4/180°C/350°F for a further 15 minutes. By this time the duck should be cooked. You can test by seeing if the juices run clear. If you prefer your duck pink in the middle, then feel free to cook it for a few minutes less.

3 Meanwhile, start the rhubarb and ginger sauce. Simmer the rhubarb with the water and sugar until it is soft and mushy – this will only take a few minutes.

4 When the duck is cooked, remove the duck from the roasting tin and keep warm. Pour out most of the juices from the roasting tin. (This fat is good for roasting potatoes.) Add the ginger to the fat left in the roasting tin, mix well and season with pepper.

5 Add the cooked rhubarb, with its juices and bring to the boil. Reduce the heat and simmer gently for about 5 minutes. Serve the sauce poured over the duck.

Mocha Lemon Curd Meringue

serves 6–8

If you have egg whites left over from another recipe, for instance the Whipped Orange Sauce (see page 109), this is a good way of using them up.

1 Whisk the egg whites until they form stiff peaks. Sprinkle in the coffee granules and add a little of the sugar. Whisk these in, then continue to whisk while gradually adding the remaining sugar. When the coffee has dissolved and the meringue is in soft peaks, it's ready.

2 Place a large piece of baking parchment on a baking sheet, then spread half of the meringue on the paper to make a circle the size of a dinner plate. I use the back of a tablespoon to do this. Repeat with the remaining meringue. You will probably need to use 2 baking sheets. Place the 2 circles in a preheated oven set at the lowest possible temperature and bake until crisp and dry. This can take up to 3 hours in my oven. When ready, peel off the baking parchment and leave to cool.

3 When you are ready to assemble the pudding, break the chocolate into small pieces and melt in a bowl over a pan of barely simmering water. Stir until smooth, and remove from the heat.

4 Place 1 meringue circle onto a platter or serving dish, and blob spoonfuls of the lemon curd on top, then spread evenly over the meringue. Spread the fromage frais over the lemon curd, then place the second meringue circle on top. Drizzle the melted chocolate in a pattern of wavy lines over the top.

3 egg whites

2 teaspoons instant coffee granules

175 g/6 oz caster sugar

50 g/2 oz dark chocolate

4 tablespoons lemon curd

200 g/7 oz fromage frais

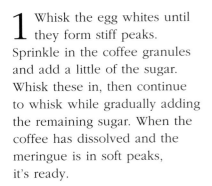

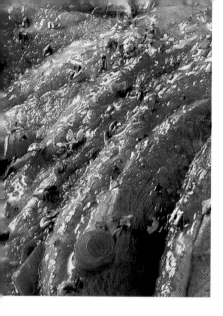

Menu 16

Hearty Duck Dish

Port-jellied Fruit Terrine

Hearty Duck Dish

serves 2

This all-in-one dish is a meal in itself. I serve it just with a simple salad of orange slices and watercress.

300 ml/½ pint lightly salted water

50 g/2 oz puy lentils

4 sun-dried tomatoes

1 teaspoon dried mixed herbs

2 duck breasts

4 small waxy potatoes, diced

1 small carrot, diced

2 fat spring onions, or ¼ onion, sliced

1 glass red wine

juice of ½ lemon

1 tablespoon chopped fresh parsley

salt and pepper

1 Heat the lightly salted water in a large saucepan and add the lentils. Bring to the boil, then reduce to a simmer.

2 Snip the sun-dried tomatoes into this, and add the dried herbs, then leave to simmer for 15 minutes.

3 Meanwhile, place the duck breasts in a roasting tin, and sprinkle generously with salt. Roast in a preheated oven at gas mark 6/200°C/400°F for 25 minutes.

4 Add the potatoes and carrot to the saucepan, and bring back up to a simmer.

5 After 25 minutes, remove the duck breasts from the roasting tin and keep warm.

6 Pour off any excess fat, leaving you with about 1 tablespoon, and add the onion. Place the tin on the hob and fry the onion for 2-3 minutes.

7 Add the wine, and season generously with pepper, but not salt, as this was added to the duck before roasting.

8 By this time, the lentil and potato mixture should be just cooked, and you can drain it if there seems to be a lot of liquid left. Add to the wine sauce, mix well and heat through until bubbling. Add the lemon juice, and check that the seasoning is to your liking.

9 Slice the duck breasts, and place on top of the lentil and potato mixture. Sprinkle over the parsley to serve.

Port-jellied Fruit Terrine

serves 6

This looks impressive, but is actually very easy to do – it just needs a bit of time and patience. It will please those of your friends who are on a diet as it is fat-free. You could use the packets of frozen fruit that are widely available, but fresh is better.

one packet (approximately 150 g/5 oz) red jelly (any flavour)

300 ml/½ pint water

300 ml/½ pint port

500 g/1 lb mixed dark red berry fruit (e.g. raspberries, redcurrants and strawberries)

1 Tear the jelly into cubes, and place in a heatproof bowl. Boil the water, then pour it over the jelly. Stir until melted. When all the jelly has melted, stir in the port.

2 Pour a little of the jelly liquid into a rectangular terrine or loaf tin, to a depth of no more than 1 cm/½ inch. Place the tin in the fridge to set. Meanwhile, keep the rest of the jelly warm so it doesn't set – placing it in a pan of hot water will do the trick.

3 Prepare the fruit by checking it over and removing any stalks. Rinse well and cut any large pieces of fruit, such as strawberries, in half.

4 When the jelly has set, place a layer of fruit over the jelly, and carefully pour some more jelly around the fruit to come no more than halfway up the fruit – if you add too much jelly, the fruit will float. Put this back in the fridge to set, then repeat until all used up. I usually do about three layers of fruit. Finish with a layer of jelly.

5 When you want to serve the terrine, dip it in a bowl of very hot water for a moment, run a knife round the edge to loosen it, and turn out upside down on a dish. Serve in slices with a little cream, if you wish.

Menu 17

Donald's Pheasant

Treacle Tart

Donald's Pheasant

serves 2–3

Pheasant can be a good, cheap meal when in season, especially if you don't mind plucking the birds yourself. This recipe uses just the best meat from the breast, and I put the rest in the stock pot. It's a good one to use when you're not sure if the meat will be from tough old birds, as the marinade tenderises them. I serve this with Brussels sprouts, mashed potatoes and parsnips for a hearty winter supper.

½ teaspoon ground ginger

2 garlic cloves, crushed

1 teaspoon walnut or olive oil

1 dessertspoon soy or Worcestershire sauce

1 rounded teaspoon dark brown sugar

150 ml/¼ pint orange juice

breasts from a brace (a pair) of pheasants

1 rounded teaspoon of arrowroot or cornflour

1 glass red wine

salt and pepper

1 Make a marinade by mixing together the ginger, garlic, walnut or olive oil, soy or Worcestershire sauce, sugar and orange juice. Put the pheasant meat in the marinade and turn it until well coated. Place in the fridge to marinate for 2 hours or more, turning at least once.

2 When you are ready to cook the dish, take the pheasant out of the marinade and place in a roasting tin. Bake in a preheated oven at gas mark 6/200°C/400°F for 15 minutes, turning once. Meanwhile, mix the arrowroot to a smooth paste with the remains of the marinade. Cornflour will thicken the juices in the same way, but does not give as nice a gloss to the finished sauce.

3 Take the cooked meat out of the roasting tin, and keep warm. Put the tin on the hob and pour in the red wine and bring to the boil, to deglaze the juices. After it has boiled for a minute or so, add the remains of the marinade with the arrowroot mixed in, bring back to the boil, and simmer until thickened.

4 Add salt and pepper to taste and pour the marinade over the pheasant to serve.

Treacle Tart

serves 4–6

I keep doing different versions of this old favourite, and at the moment this seems the best, which isn't to say I won't do it differently next time. This version is rather nice though, as the sharpness of the grated apple offsets the sweetness of the syrup.

1 Lightly grease a round pie dish (about 20 cm/8 inches in diameter), and roll out about ⅔ of the pastry on a floured surface. Use this to line the tin, and keep the trimmings.

2 Mix together the sultanas, apple, lemon zest and juice, breadcrumbs and syrup. Gently spread this mixture over the pastry base.

3 Roll out the rest of the pastry and cut it into thin strips, and use these strips to make a lattice topping for the pie, crossing them and twisting if you wish. Fasten the strips to the rim of the tart with a little water.

4 Bake the tart in a preheated oven at gas mark 7/220°C/425°F for 10 minutes, then turn the oven down to gas mark 4/180°C/350°F for a further 20 minutes. This is delicious served either hot or cold – but you have to have a sweet tooth!

butter, for greasing

flour, for dusting

375 g/12 oz shortcrust pastry

125 g/4 oz sultanas

1 large cooking apple, grated

grated zest and juice of ½ lemon

50 g/2 oz breadcrumbs

125 g/4 oz golden syrup

Note

A handy tip: To make measuring golden syrup easier, first warm the syrup by standing the tin in a bowl of hot water. This slightly melts the syrup, making life much easier!

Menu 18

Sausage and Pâté Plait

Garlic Cabbage

Shirley's Caramel Cream

Sausage and Pâté Plait

serves 4

They say that a cauliflower is an educated cabbage – well then, this recipe is for a sausage roll that has been to college. The addition of the pâté and vegetables to the basic sausage meat makes the filling that bit more interesting, and the strip effect of the pastry makes for a smart finish.

We have this warm with vegetables for a family meal, but cold can make a nice addition to a picnic or buffet table.

375 g/12 oz puff pastry

500 g/1 lb pork sausage meat

150 g/5 oz smooth pork or chicken liver pâté

2 tomatoes, chopped

½ bunch spring onions, trimmed and sliced

flour, for dusting

a little milk, to glaze

1 Roll out the pastry on a well-floured surface to make a rectangle about 30 x 38 cm/ 12 x 15 inches.

2 Place the sausage meat, pâté, tomatoes and spring onions in a large bowl, and mix together. I find this easiest to do with my hands.

3 Spread this mixture down the centre third of the rolled out pastry, but leave approximately 2 cm/1 inch around the edges of the pastry.

4 With a sharp knife, make a series of cuts from the filling to the edge of the pastry on the long sides, making sure that the cuts are matched on either side.

5 Brush a little milk down the cut edges, then fold over the top and bottom edges. Fold over strips of pastry from the sides to cover the filling, alternating from each side. The strips should overlap.

6 Brush all over the plait with more milk, and place on a greased baking sheet. Bake in a preheated oven at gas mark 6/ 200°C/400°F for 30 minutes, until the pastry is crisp and golden brown. To serve, slice into 8, and give each person 2 slices.

Garlic Cabbage

serves 4–6

I'm giving a recipe here for something I have never cooked. I'm sure it's right, as I've eaten it many times and I followed my husband round the kitchen with a pencil and paper last time he made it, and wrote it all down. My theory is – let people do what they're good at and don't interfere – just enjoy the results! This is an ideal vegetable accompaniment for strong-tasting meats.

1 Cut the cabbage into quarters and discard the stalk. Grate or chop the cabbage – you can chop it by hand, but I find it much easier to use the coarsest grater setting on a food processor.

2 Drop the cabbage into a pan of lightly salted, boiling water, and boil for 1½ minutes only – please don't overcook this – time it very carefully. Tip the cabbage into a colander or sieve, and press out as much water as you can with the back of a wooden spoon.

3 Rinse out the pan, then add the butter and garlic. When the butter has melted, and the garlic is just starting to soften, add the drained cabbage with a generous seasoning of pepper. Stir-fry for 1 minute, then turn into a warmed dish and serve.

750 g/1½ lb hard white cabbage (discard the outer leaves)

50 g/2 oz butter

2 garlic cloves, crushed

salt and pepper

Menu 18

Shirley's Caramel Cream

serves 4

As she has a big family, Shirley usually makes double quantities of this classic pudding in one large dish. I've given amounts for 4, and it looks nice made in small dishes or tea cups for individual portions. Either way, it's a smooth, delicious treat that can be made 1-2 days in advance.

5 tablespoons water

175 g /6 oz granulated sugar

600 ml/1 pint milk

1 vanilla pod or 1 teaspoon vanilla extract

2 eggs

2 egg yolks

1 To make the caramel, heat the water and 100 g/3½ oz of the sugar together gently, until the sugar has dissolved, then boil steadily until it turns a golden brown. Pour into the base of a small ovenproof dish (or 4 small ramekin dishes) and turn so the base is well covered. It's fine if the caramel comes up the sides a little. Leave to cool and set.

2 To make the cream, heat the milk in a saucepan with the vanilla pod (if using), until almost at boiling point, then leave to cool for 10 minutes. When the milk has cooled, remove the vanilla pod. (You can re-use the vanilla pod if you rinse and dry it afterwards.) If using vanilla extract, add when the milk has cooled for 10 minutes.

3 Whisk the eggs and egg yolks together, then add the remaining sugar and whisk again until paler in colour. Stir in the milk (which will still be just warm), and mix thoroughly.

4 Pour this mixture through a sieve to remove any threads from the eggs, then carefully pour it into the dish containing the caramel. I suggest you pour the mixture over the back of a spoon to help control the flow, and to not disturb the caramel.

5 Place your dish in a roasting tin, then pour around hot water to come about halfway up the sides of the dish. Bake in a preheated oven at gas mark 4/180°C/350°F for 40-50 minutes. To test if done, insert the blade of a knife in the centre, and if it comes out clean, it is ready. Leave to cool completely.

6 To serve, run a knife around the edge of the dish and place a serving plate over the top. Carefully turn upside-down.

Menu 19

New Bangers and Mash

Roasted Red Onion Gravy

Autumn Pudding

New Bangers and Mash

serves 4

Fashions in food are very strange. Bangers and mash used to be old-fashioned, working class food, but with the 80s revival of interest in traditional British dishes, tarted-up versions of the old favourites began to appear on the menus of smart restaurants, often with a special little twist added by an enthusiastic young chef. Specialist sausage shops have appeared too, selling more varieties than you would think possible. I must say that I like the meaty, butcher's best, traditional pork sausage, but my favourite of all is a coil of Cumberland sausage, nicely herbed and spiced.

I like Brussels sprouts with this in the winter, and peas in the summer months.

1 kg /2 lbs potatoes, peeled and cut into even-sized chunks

500 g/1 lb parsnips, peeled and cut into even-sized chunks

1 kg/2 lbs sausages

a knob of butter

3 tablespoons top-of-the-milk or single cream

chopped parsley, to serve

salt

1 Boil the potatoes and the parsnips in lightly salted water for 20 minutes.

2 Meanwhile, grill or bake the sausages until well-browned on all sides.

3 Drain the potatoes and parsnips, then add the butter and top-of-the-milk or single cream. Mash together thoroughly using a potato masher. When there are no lumps left, fluff up by beating vigorously with a fork.

4 Season with a little more salt if you wish, then sprinkle with plenty of chopped parsley.

Roasted Red Onion Gravy

makes 300 ml/½ pint

1 Place the onions in a roasting tin and drizzle the oil over. Roast in a preheated oven at gas mark 6/200°C/400°F for 15 minutes, turning a couple of times during the cooking time.

2 Remove the tin from the oven and place it on the hob over a medium heat. Mix the stock with the herbs, then pour over the roasted onions.

3 Mix the cornflour to a smooth paste with a little water, then add to the onions and stock. Bring to the boil, then simmer until thickened to your liking. Season to taste.

2 red onions, sliced thickly

1 tablespoon olive oil

450 ml/¾ pint vegetable stock

½ teaspoon dried mixed herbs

2 rounded teaspoons cornflour

salt and pepper

Autumn Pudding

serves 6

This is a new version of an old favourite – Summer Pudding. This one uses the more mature flavours of later in the year, with just a touch of warming spice.

1 Use scissors to cut the fruit into even-sized pieces. An apricot half, cut in half again, is roughly the size to aim for.

2 Place the fruit in a pan with the sugar, water and cinnamon, bring to the boil and simmer for about 10 minutes, until the fruit is soft.

3 Meanwhile, line a 900 ml/1½ pint pudding basin with clingfilm, leaving a generous overlap – this makes it easier to turn the pudding out. Use the bread to line the base and sides of the bowl. Cut the bread with scissors or a knife to make sure it fits the bowl well, without leaving any gaps.

4 Spoon the warm fruit into the basin, reserving some of the juice, filling it to near the top of the bread. Press the fruit down.

5 Use the rest of the bread to make a lid, and fold over the clingfilm to help keep the shape of the pudding.

6 Choose a plate that just fits inside the bowl, and place it on top. Put a weight or a heavy tin on top, and place in the fridge overnight.

7 When ready to serve, remove the weight and plate, and use the clingfilm to help you turn out the pudding onto another plate. Use the reserved juice to moisten any parts of the bread not fully soaked in juice.

500 g/1 lb dried fruit mixture (e.g. apricots, figs, apple slices and sultanas)

75 g/3 oz brown sugar

300 ml/½ pint water

½ teaspoon ground cinnamon

300 g/10 oz sliced brown bread, crusts removed

Menu 20

Roasted Bacon

Old-fashioned Apricot Tart

Roasted Bacon

serves 6

I serve this with green vegetables such as broad beans or peas and Crisp Roast Potatoes (see page 114). It is also good cold, served with fruity relishes and pickles.

1 × 1 kg/2 lb joint of bacon

about 15 cloves

1 tablespoon dark brown sugar

1 tablespoon French mustard

2 garlic cloves, crushed, or 5 cm/2 inches garlic purée

1 Soak the bacon in a bowl of cold water for several hours, or overnight. Drain, then pat dry. Score through the surface of the meat in a diamond pattern using a sharp knife. Push the cloves into the crossover points – make the points deeper with the point of the knife, if necessary.

2 Mix together the sugar, mustard and garlic to make a paste. Spread this over the meat among the cloves, and place in a roasting tin.

3 Roast the bacon in a preheated oven at gas mark 6/200°C/400°F for 40 minutes. I base this cooking time on 20 minutes per 500 g/1 lb, so adjust the cooking time if your joint is a different size.

4 Remove the joint from the tin, and leave it to stand for 5-10 minutes before serving. This will make the joint easier to carve.

5 If you like, use the roasting juices to make a gravy. Simply add a little stock or vegetable water and perhaps a glass of port. Season with black pepper, but don't add any salt – the bacon will be salty enough. Cook the gravy over the hob, stirring all the time, until reduced to the consistency you like. Pour into a warmed gravy boat.

Old-fashioned Apricot Tart

serves 6

This recipe is based on one from the late, great, Jane Grigson – a most learned and practical champion of our traditional food. She would have used fresh apricots, but these are not always available, and the ready-to-eat dried ones have an excellent flavour and are packed with good things, such as betacarotene. The pastry is actually more like cake, as it is enriched with eggs and sugar.

1 First make the pastry. Mix together the white and wholemeal flour, sugar and a pinch of salt, and rub in the butter. You can do this by hand, but I use a food processor.

2 Add the egg and mix to make a soft dough. (I drop the egg into the food processor as it is running, and it does the work for you.)

3 You could roll out the pastry on a well-floured surface, but it is so soft that you can just press it into the tin. Grease a round, loose-based tin (I like to use one with fluted edges, about 24 cm/9½ inches in diameter), and using your fingers, press the pastry into the tin, covering the base and sides. Place in the fridge to chill.

4 Line the pastry with foil and 'bake blind' (this means without a filling) in a preheated oven at gas mark 6/200°C/400°F for 10 minutes. Remove the foil and bake for a further 5 minutes. This sets the pastry without browning it too much.

5 Meanwhile, make the filling. Heat the sugar and water together gently until the sugar has melted, then add the apricots and bring to the boil. Reduce the heat and simmer gently for 10 minutes. Remove the apricots with a slotted spoon and leave to cool.

6 Reduce the cooking liquid by boiling for about 10 minutes until you have a thick, syrupy glaze, and keep it warm while you do steps 7 and 8.

7 Arrange the cooled apricots in the pastry case, still within the tin. I like to arrange them in concentric circles.

8 Beat together the eggs, crème fraîche and the tablespoon of caster sugar, then pour in the melted butter and mix well. Pour this over the apricots carefully so as not to disturb them, and return the tart to the oven for a further 20 minutes. The filling will be almost set – if it still seems wobbly, cook for a further 5 minutes.

9 Leave to cool for a little to set further, then drizzle some of the syrupy glaze over the top. You could chill before serving, but it tastes especially good if slightly warm.

FOR THE PASTRY:

75 g/3 oz white self-raising flour

75 g/3 oz wholemeal self-raising flour

1 dessertspoon caster sugar

75 g/3 oz butter (cold from the fridge), plus extra for greasing

1 small egg, beaten

flour, for dusting (optional)

salt

FOR THE FILLING:

150 g/5 oz caster sugar

300 ml/½ pint water

500 g/1 lb ready-to-eat dried apricots

2 eggs

300 ml/½ pint crème fraîche

1 tablespoon caster sugar

25 g/1 oz butter, melted

Menu 21

Gammon with an Orange Mustard Sauce

Cherry Batter Pudding

Gammon with an Orange Mustard Sauce

serves 2

As a lot of people like mustard with their ham, I've put some in the sauce here, and it works well. Try serving lightly cooked Savoy cabbage or spring greens with this.

1 tablespoon oil

2 teaspoons mild wholegrain mustard

2 large slices gammon, approximately 170g/6 oz each

grated zest and juice of 1 large orange

pepper

chopped fresh parsley, to serve

1 Heat the oil in the base of a large frying pan (use one that has a lid).

2 Smear half the mustard over one side of each piece of gammon, then lay in the pan mustard side down. Smear the remaining mustard over the top of the gammon.

3 Fry over a high heat for 2-3 minutes on each side, then add the orange juice.

4 Put the lid on, and leave to simmer for 5 minutes, turning once.

5 Season with pepper (don't add salt, as the gammon will be salty enough). Stir in the orange zest, then serve the gammon with the sauce poured over the meat. Sprinkle over some chopped fresh parsley, to serve.

Cherry Batter Pudding

serves 4–6

1 Make a sweet batter by combining the milk, eggs, sugar, salt and the flour – I usually do this in a food processor, but if you do this by hand, whisk the milk and eggs together, then continue whisking while gradually adding the dry ingredients. Leave the batter to stand for ½ hour, to thicken nicely.

2 Grease a round, shallow, ovenproof dish (about 23 cm/9 inches in diameter), and scatter the cherries over the base.

3 Pour the batter over the cherries, and bake in a preheated oven at gas mark 6/200°C/400°F for about ½ hour, until golden brown at the edges and just set.

300 ml/½ pint milk

2 eggs

2 tablespoons caster sugar

a pinch of salt

125 g/4 oz white plain flour

butter, for greasing

500 g/1 lb cherries, stones and stalks removed

Note

For a variation, you could make 4-6 small puddings. Make as for 1 large pudding, but use muffin tins. Bake at the same temperature but for slightly less time – about 20 minutes will be enough.

Menu 22

Pork Ribs with a Spicy Apricot Sauce
Berry Pudding

Pork Ribs with a Spicy Apricot Sauce

serves 4

This has a sweet-and-sour flavour with a bit of a spicy kick, so I like to serve it with plain boiled rice mixed with peas and sweetcorn.

2 tablespoons vegetable oil

1 large onion, chopped

2 garlic cloves, crushed

125 g/4 oz ready-to-eat dried apricots, chopped

a dash of Tabasco sauce

1 dessertspoon Worcestershire sauce

1 tablespoon red wine vinegar

3 tablespoons apricot jam

150 ml/¼ pint cider

1 kg/2 lb pork ribs

1 Heat the oil in a pan, add the onion and the garlic, and fry for a few minutes, until softened and starting to brown.

2 Add the apricots, Tabasco and Worcestershire sauces, vinegar, jam and cider. Cover, and simmer for 5 minutes, until the apricot pieces have softened.

3 Pour this hot mixture over the ribs, and leave for ½ hour to marinate, covered, in a cool place.

4 Take the meat out of the marinade and grill under a moderate, preheated grill for about 10 minutes on each side. Check that the meat is cooked through, and not just on the outside. Baste with a little of the marinade during cooking to stop the ribs burning.

5 Meanwhile, use the remaining marinade to make the sauce. Transfer to a saucepan, bring up to the boil and cook for about 3 minutes, adding a little water if it seems too thick. Serve poured over the ribs.

Berry Pudding

serves 4

You can use bilberries or blueberries in this recipe, but if you are lucky enough to have a blackcurrant bush in your garden, or your supermarket stocks them, the deep colour and flavour of the ripe berries will be ideal. You need to start this recipe the day before you want to serve it.

200 g/7 oz dark berry fruit, plus extra for decoration

125 g/4 oz caster sugar

2 tablespoons port

300 ml/½ pint double cream

1 The day before you want to serve this pudding, whizz the berries and sugar together in a blender or food processor until the sugar melts into the juice, then pour through a sieve, catching the juice in a bowl. Discard the pips.

2 Stir the port into the juice, then leave the bowl covered in the fridge or in a cool larder until the next day, when the mixture will have thickened and gelled.

3 Whip the cream until thick and floppy, then fold the fruit mixture into the cream. Pile into stemmed glass dishes to serve, decorated with the extra berries.

Menu 23

Pork Collops

Baked Pears in Almond Meringue

Pork Collops

serves 2

This is similar to Wiener schnitzel, but uses pork rather than veal. It's a tasty way of using pork, but will also suit those who find veal expensive, or who dislike the way veal is reared. Serve this with a green vegetable – I like it with green beans or peas.

2 pork steaks or loin, approximately 150 g/5 oz each

2 tablespoons paprika

½ lemon

1 egg

50 g/2 oz breadcrumbs

1 tablespoon vegetable oil

15 g/½ oz butter

1 Trim off any fat from the meat and use a flat wooden mallet or rolling pin to beat it out to about double its original size – this is easiest to do with the pork placed between 2 sheets of clingfilm.

2 Season each side of the meat with the paprika.

3 Cut a large slice from the lemon, cut it in half, and reserve for decoration. Squeeze the juice from the remaining piece of lemon, add the egg and beat together.

4 Spread the breadcrumbs on a plate, and heat the oil and butter in a large frying pan. Dip the pork into the egg and lemon mixture to coat, then into the breadcrumbs, patting them so the pork is well sealed.

5 Place the pork into the hot oil and butter, and cook over a medium heat for about 5 minutes on each side, until crisp and golden brown and with the meat cooked through. To test, push a knife into the thickest part of the meat – the knife will go in easily if the pork is done, and the juices should run clear.

Baked Pears in Almond Meringue

serves 4

I like to use Williams pears (the short fat ones) for this recipe, but any will do, as long as they are not too soft, as the baking softens them further. Amaretto (a brand of almond liqueur) goes wonderfully with the flavour of ground almonds, but any liqueur will work – I've used Cointreau or brandy at times. Have a look at what you have in the cupboard left over from Christmas!

4 pears, peeled, halved and cored

2 tablespoons ground almonds

4 tablespoons cream cheese

2 tablespoons Amaretto or other liqueur

2 egg whites

125 g/4 oz caster sugar

25 g/1 oz toasted flaked almonds

Note
The easiest way to peel pears is using a swivel potato peeler. This wastes very little, and can be used to gouge out the cores easily, too.

1 Lay the pears cored-side up in a round, ovenproof dish (about 22 cm/8½ inches in diameter) to make a circle, with the pointed ends facing inwards.

2 Put the ground almonds, cream cheese and Amaretto or other liqueur into a bowl and mix together with a wooden spoon until well combined and soft.

3 Whisk the egg whites in another bowl until stiff, then gradually whisk in the sugar until stiff and glossy.

4 Using a metal spoon, gently fold the cream cheese mixture into the meringue.

5 Pile the meringue into the centre of the dish of pears, leaving the edges of the pears showing round the sides of the dish. Scatter the flaked almonds over the top.

6 Bake in a preheated oven at gas mark 6/200°C/400°F for 15-20 minutes, or until the meringue mixture is crisp and golden brown on top. Serve immediately.

Menu 24

Bacon and Beans

Ripon Cheese and Apple Pie

Bacon and Beans

serves 4

I serve this with a green salad and chunks of French bread to soak up the juices.

1 tablespoon oil

1 large onion, chopped

2 garlic cloves, crushed

250 g/8 oz bacon, cut into small pieces

2 U-shaped, cooked, smoked sausages, sliced

2 tablespoons tomato purée

1 bay leaf

2 tins (approximately 425g/ 14 oz each) haricot or cannellini beans, rinsed

300 ml/½ pint boiling water

salt and pepper

1 Heat the oil in a large, deep frying pan, and fry the onion and garlic until the onion starts to soften. Add the bacon and fry until crisp.

2 Add the sausages, tomato purée, bay leaf and beans and mix together.

3 Add the water and bring to a simmer. Simmer for at least 5 minutes so the flavours mingle, and stir occasionally but not too vigorously, as this will break up the beans.

4 Season to taste – you will probably find that you won't need to add any salt, as the bacon may be salty enough.

Ripon Cheese and Apple Pie

serves 8

We often have a wedge of cheese with apple pie or fruitcake, so perhaps it isn't surprising to find a recipe that bakes apple and cheese together. In fact, this has been happening in Yorkshire for quite a while – this was said to be made originally for Saint Wilfrid when he returned to Ripon from Rome. It also neatly solves the dilemma of pudding or cheese – this way, everyone can have both!

375 g/12 oz white plain flour, plus extra for dusting

a pinch of salt

175 g/6 oz hard margarine, cut into pieces, plus extra for greasing

1 kg/2 lbs cooking apples, peeled, cored and sliced thickly

125 g/4 oz caster sugar, plus extra for sprinkling

175 g/6 oz Wensleydale cheese

a little milk, for brushing

1 First, make the pastry: sieve the flour and salt together, then rub in the margarine until the mixture resembles fine breadcrumbs. Use a fork to work in just enough cold water to bind it into a soft, but not sticky, dough.

2 Grease a baking tin (I use a Swiss roll tin, which is about 20 x 25 cm/8 x 10 inches), and divide the pastry into 2, with one piece slightly larger than the other. Roll out the larger piece on a floured surface to make a rectangle that will cover the base and sides of the tin. Lay the pastry in without stretching, and trim the edges.

3 Spread the apple slices over the pastry base in an even layer, then sprinkle the sugar over them.

4 Grate or crumble the cheese (whichever seems easiest), and spread this evenly over the apples.

5 Brush the edges of the pastry base with a little water. Roll out the remaining pastry to make a rectangle that will fit as a lid, and place the lid on top. To get a good seal, pinch the edges together using a finger and thumb to make a wavy pattern all round.

6 Make a double row of small slits in the top of the pastry with the point of a sharp knife, then brush the top of the pastry with a little milk. Sprinkle over some extra caster sugar.

7 Bake in a preheated oven at gas mark 6/200°C/400°F for about 30 minutes, until the pastry is crisp and golden. Serve warm or cold, cut into slices.

Menu 25

Peppered Beef and Bacon Rolls

Flambéed Fruits

Fudge Sauce

Peppered Beef and Bacon Rolls

serves 2

You might find that you need to trim or stretch your slices of beef and bacon in order that the bacon is slightly smaller than the beef. Lightly steamed carrot and courgette ribbons go well with this.

4 rashers streaky bacon

4 thin slices beef steak (about 250 g/8 oz in total)

1 tablespoon white plain flour

2 teaspoons oil

½ onion, chopped

1 medium carrot, diced

1 teaspoon dried mixed herbs

1 glass red wine

150 ml/¼ pint beef stock

salt and pepper

1 Lay a rasher of bacon on top of each slice of beef, then roll up each slice of beef, with the bacon inside.

2 Sprinkle the flour on a plate and season liberally with pepper. Roll each beef and bacon roll in the flour until well coated, then fasten with a cocktail stick.

3 Heat the oil in a flameproof casserole dish on the hob, and cook the rolls until browned on 2 sides.

4 Add the onion and carrot and sprinkle over the herbs. Pour over the wine and stock, and bring to the boil. Turn the heat down to a simmer and

place the lid on the dish. Cook for 30 minutes to 1 hour (the cooking time depends upon the sort of beef used – braising steak will take longer than a more expensive cut such as rump). Test with a knife to see when the beef is tender.

5 When the rolls are cooked, taste the gravy, and season with salt and pepper to taste – remember that bacon is salty, so you may not need to add any extra salt.

6 Serve the rolls with the gravy poured over. It's up to you whether you remove the skewers, or if you leave them for people to remove themselves.

Flambéed Fruits

serves 4

It's best to use three fruits for this. I use plums, nectarines, and bananas, but you can vary the fruit according to what is available. This is great served with Fudge Sauce, but you could try it with ice cream or cream.

1 Brush the base of a heavy frying pan, preferably a griddle pan with ridges on the base, with a little butter, then heat it and lightly toast the fruit on two sides.

2 Pour the brandy over the fruit, then, keeping your head well back, ignite the brandy. Serve immediately.

butter, for greasing

2 bananas, cut into 4 pieces

4 plums, halved and stoned

2 nectarines, quartered and stoned

2 tablespoons brandy

Fudge Sauce

serves 6

This sauce is excellent with ice cream, and will keep in a jar in the fridge for a week or more.

1 Place the butter, sugar and double cream in a small pan, and heat gently until the butter has melted.

2 Increase the heat to a simmer, and simmer together for 2 minutes, stirring continuously. Serve immediately, but if you are not using this straight away, you need to reheat the sauce to simmering point before serving.

125 g/4 oz butter

200 g/7 oz dark brown soft sugar

1 small carton (approximately 150 ml/¼ pint) double cream

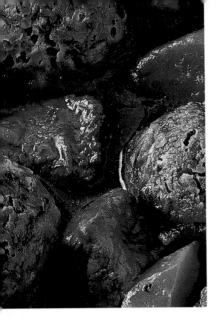

Menu 26

Beef Stew with Dumplings

Gooseberry and Elderflower Fool

Beef Stew with Dumplings

serves 4

FOR THE STEW:

2 tablespoons white plain flour

750 g/1½ lb stewing beef, cut into cubes

1 tablespoon oil

1 large onion, chopped

3 large carrots, chopped

1 teaspoon dried mixed herbs

1 tablespoon tomato purée

1 teaspoon Worcestershire sauce

600 ml/1 pint beef stock

FOR THE DUMPLINGS:

125 g/4 oz white self-raising flour

50 g/2 oz shredded suet

1 tablespoon chopped fresh parsley

salt and pepper

This is a hearty, warming dish, ideal for a cold day. Dumplings were a popular way of making a bit of expensive meat go further, but we don't seem to make them much these days. They are very quick and easy to make, and are guaranteed to fill you up. Serve with some lightly boiled or steamed broccoli.

1 Season the flour, then toss the meat in the flour to coat. An easy way to do this is to place the beef and flour in a polythene bag. Shake well to coat the beef.

2 Heat the oil in a flameproof casserole and fry the onion until it starts to brown. Add the floured meat and stir to coat in the hot oil and onion.

3 Add the carrot, mixed herbs, tomato purée, Worcestershire sauce and stock and mix well.

4 You can either cook this on the hob, or in an oven. Put the lid on the casserole and either bring to the boil and

simmer, or cook in a preheated oven at gas mark 4/180°C/350°F until the meat is tender, stirring from time to time. It will take between 1½-2 hours, depending on your cooking method. Add a little more water if necessary.

5 To make the dumplings, mix together the flour, suet and parsley. Season, and add just enough cold water to make a soft dough.

6 Roll the dough into small balls, and add to the casserole about 20 minutes before the end of the cooking time. Remove the casserole lid for the last 5 minutes so the dumplings go brown and slightly crisp on top.

Gooseberry and Elderflower Fool

serves 6

If you have gooseberries to pick when the elder is in full flower, then jolly good – I've never managed it yet! The gooseberries generally appear later, so I use elderflower cordial to add a wonderful, fresh, summery tang. If you have elderberries, use a few instead of the cordial. A viewer sent in a helpful tip – use nail clippers to top and tail the gooseberries – make sure you wash your clippers first!

750 g /1½ lbs gooseberries

170 g/6 oz caster sugar, plus extra, to taste

1 tablespoon elderflower cordial

150 ml/¼ pint double cream

150 ml/¼ pint thick custard

1 Top and tail the gooseberries and put them in a pan with about 2 tablespoons of water – you want just enough water to cook the gooseberries, without burning them. Simmer gently until all the berries have burst and the skins are soft, then set aside to cool.

2 When cool, mash the gooseberries together with the sugar and elderflower cordial. Taste the mixture, and if you like, add a little more sugar if necessary.

3 Gently fold in the cream, followed by the custard, to create a ripple effect. You should still be able to see all the different colours. Spoon into 6 stemmed glasses and serve chilled.

Menu 27

Braised Venison Steaks

Chestnut Croquettes

Peach Frangipane

Braised Venison Steaks

serves 2

Serve with lightly steamed seasonal vegetables.

125 g/4 oz mushrooms, chopped

3 large or 6 small spring onions, finely chopped

1-2 garlic cloves, crushed

2 glasses red wine

2 venison steaks, approximately 175 g/6 oz each

1 tablespoon oil

1 rounded tablespoon redcurrant jelly

2 teaspoons arrowroot or cornflour

1 teaspoon celery salt

2 tablespoons water

pepper

1 Put the mushrooms, spring onions, garlic and red wine in a large bowl, and season with pepper. Mix well, and put the venison steaks in to marinate for several hours if possible, turning at least once.

2 When you are ready to cook the dish, remove the venison. Heat the oil in a frying pan (use one that has a lid), and brown the venison over a high heat for 2 minutes on each side.

3 Add the remains of the marinade to the pan, bring to the boil, then reduce the heat. Cover and simmer for 10 minutes, turning the venison once during this time.

4 Remove the meat, and keep warm on a serving dish. Add the redcurrant jelly and boil for 5 minutes, by which time the sauce will have reduced and the jelly dissolved into it.

5 Mix the arrowroot or cornflour and celery salt together to a smooth paste with the water, then add this to the sauce, stirring all the time, and bring to the boil. Simmer for 2-3 minutes until thickened, then serve poured over the venison steaks.

Chestnut Croquettes

serves 2

Cooked, whole chestnuts are sold vacuum-packed, or you can get them tinned, in salted water. These croquettes can be made in advance and kept warm until needed.

1 tablespoon chopped fresh herbs (I like to use thyme, chives, or a mixture of both)

275 g/9 oz cooked, whole chestnuts

1 small egg

flour, for dusting

oil, for frying

salt and pepper

1 Put the herbs and chestnuts in a food processor and season well. Using a metal blade, whizz together until they resemble fine breadcrumbs.

2 With the food processor still running, add the egg. The mixture will bind together into a ball.

3 On a well-floured surface, with floured hands, form the mixture into 4 croquettes or patties. Heat enough oil in a deep frying pan to shallow fry the croquettes, then fry for about 10 minutes, turning, until crisp and brown on all sides.

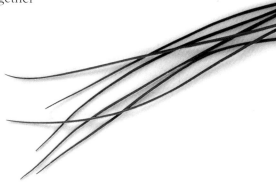

Peach Frangipane

serves 6

You can make this with any kind of jam, but my family likes the sort of peach jam that has chunks in it, and the flavour goes really well with the almonds.

1 Roll out about two-thirds of the pastry on a well-floured surface to make a circle big enough to cover the base and sides of a round pie dish (about 20 cm/8 inches in diameter).

2 Lightly grease the dish, then fit the pastry in. Trim the edges, and keep the trimmings. Spread the peach jam evenly over the pastry base.

3 Cream together the butter and sugar in a bowl until it goes pale and fluffy.

4 Beat the eggs together, and gradually beat into the creamed mixture.

5 Stir in the ground almonds, and spread this mixture over the jam, smoothing it level with a spatula.

6 Roll out the rest of the pastry and cut it into thin strips. Use these strips to make a lattice topping for the pie, crossing them and twisting if you wish. Fasten them to the edges of the tart with a little water.

7 Bake in a preheated oven at gas mark 5/190°C/375°F for 50 minutes, by which time the filling should be just about set and golden brown. It will set a little more, and sink a bit, as it cools. We like this served just warm, with custard or single cream.

375 g/12 oz puff pastry

flour, for dusting

3-4 tablespoons peach jam

125 g/4 oz butter, softened, plus extra for greasing

125 g/4 oz caster sugar

2 large eggs

125 g/4 oz ground almonds

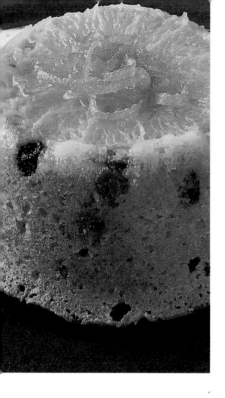

Menu 28

Roast Goose

Gooseberry Sauce

Apple Stuffing

Light Mincemeat Puddings

Whipped Orange Sauce

Goose cooking time

I have given you the cooking time for a 4.5 kg/10 lb goose, so if you are cooking a different size, follow this timing: 20 minutes for each 500 g/1 lb + 30 minutes. Leave to stand for 20 minutes.

Roast Goose

serves 6

Geese are deceptive. Like ducks, they have a bigger, squarer frame than chickens or turkeys, and you can look at a bird that you think might serve 6, and it will only do 4. You will need a 4.5 kg/10 lb goose to feed 6.

Goose is very rich, which means that the lean meat has fat in it, as well as the fat you can see, so to get the best results cook it on a rack as I have done here. This ensures that the fat flows away from the bird and into the roasting tin, otherwise it may be too fatty for our modern tastes. The fat is by far the best for roast potatoes, so make sure you keep it. It will last for weeks if kept in the fridge. A good vegetable to serve with Roast Goose would be leeks, simply cleaned, sliced into rings, and simmered for 5 minutes in lightly salted water. Drain well before serving. By the way, there is no need to peel the onion and apple first.

1 Stuff the onion and apple pieces into the body cavity of the goose, both in the front and back.

2 Prick the goose all over with a sharp skewer, and rub salt and pepper over the skin.

3 Cover the legs (which tend to burn if not covered), with a double wrapping of foil. Place a rack inside your largest roasting tray, then place the goose on the rack, breast side up. Cover the goose and rack with a large piece of foil.

4 Roast in a preheated oven at gas mark 6/200°C/400°F for 3 hours and 50 minutes. You will need to 'rest' the goose for 20 minutes before serving to make it easier to carve, and more tender, so be sure to take this into account when you are working out when to serve it.

5 After an hour, take the goose out of the oven, and turn it over. Re-cover with the foil, and put back in the oven to continue cooking.

6 For the last 45 minutes, turn the goose back to breast side up, and roast it without the foil covering so that the breast goes golden brown – keep an eye on it, and cover with foil if it is browning too much. You may need to pour off some of the surplus fat from the tin.

7 To check whether the goose is cooked, pierce the thickest part with a skewer. If the juices run clear, it is cooked. Leave the goose to stand on a warmed serving dish, for 20 minutes or so before carving.

1 onion, quartered

1 cooking apple, quartered

1 × 4.5 kg /10 lb goose

salt and pepper

Gooseberry Sauce

serves 6–8

Fresh gooseberries are in the shops for only a short time in the summer, and if you can remember to make some gooseberry sauce with them and freeze it ready for winter, that's ideal. If not, buy frozen gooseberries rather than tinned. Serve warm with any rich roast meat – it is particularly good with goose or duck.

500 g/1 lb gooseberries

1-3 tablespoons water

50 g/2 oz butter

125 g/4 oz caster sugar

1 Place the gooseberries and some water in a pan and heat gently until simmering. Fresh gooseberries will need about 3 tablespoons of water, whereas frozen or tinned ones will only need 1 tablespoon of water. Cook until soft, stirring occasionally. Fresh gooseberries will take about 10 minutes to cook, frozen or tinned will take about 5 minutes.

2 Tip the gooseberries into a sieve over a bowl, and push through with the back of a wooden spoon – this will leave you with a smooth fruit purée without pips.

3 Rinse out the pan, and put the gooseberry purée back in it. Add the butter and sugar, and warm through over a gentle heat, stirring, until the sugar and butter have melted.

Apple Stuffing

serves 6

This is a favourite of ours, and it works very well with the Roast Goose and Gooseberry Sauce. You can cook this inside the goose, but I think it is better cooked separately.

1 Peel, core and quarter the apples. Slice them into a bowl, and pour the rum over the top to prevent them from going brown. Mix to coat in the rum, then put aside to soak for as long as you can, but for at least 3 hours.

2 Mix together the eggs, sage, nutmeg, salt and the breadcrumbs.

3 Stir this mixture into the rum-soaked apples, then tip it into a greased ovenproof dish. Bake in a preheated oven at gas mark 6/200°C/400°F for 15 minutes, until the surface is crisp.

750 g /1½ lb eating apples

175 ml/6 fl oz dark rum

2 eggs, beaten

8 sage leaves, chopped

2 teaspoons ground nutmeg

a pinch of salt

500 g/1 lb brown breadcrumbs

Light Mincemeat Puddings

serves 6

This is lovely with the Whipped Orange Sauce, but it's also good served with cream.

1 First, grate the zest from the orange, and keep this to add to the pudding mixture.

2 You will need 6 small pudding bowls or ramekin dishes (about 8 cm/3 inches in diameter). To prepare the bowls, start by cutting off the remaining peel and pith using a small serrated knife. Cut the orange into 6 slices. Brush the inside of the ramekin dishes or pudding bowls with a little melted butter. Sprinkle in a little caster sugar, and shake until the butter is coated. Shake out any excess sugar, then place a slice of orange in the bottom of each dish or bowl.

3 To make the puddings, first cream the butter with half of the caster sugar until pale and fluffy.

4 Beat the egg yolks one by one into the creamed mixture, adding 1 teaspoon of cake crumbs if the mixture seems in danger of curdling.

5 Add the rest of the crumbs together with the cinnamon and mincemeat and mix well.

6 In another bowl, whisk the egg whites until they form soft peaks, then gradually whisk in the remaining caster sugar.

7 Fold the mincemeat mixture into the meringue, very gently, so as not to lose any of the air.

8 Divide the mixture between the prepared bowls, and place them in a large roasting tray. Carefully pour boiling water around the bowls until about 2 cm/1 inch deep. Bake in a preheated oven at gas mark 4/180°C/350°F for 25 minutes. To serve, run a knife round the edge of each bowl to loosen before turning out, upside-down.

TO PREPARE THE BOWLS:

1 orange

a little melted butter

a little caster sugar

FOR THE MINCEMEAT PUDDINGS:

50 g/2 oz butter, softened

50 g/2 oz caster sugar

3 eggs, separated

75 g/3 oz trifle sponge, or plain Madeira cake, crumbled

½ teaspoon ground cinnamon

75 g/3 oz mincemeat

Note
These puddings can be made in advance, and reheated, and can also be frozen. To reheat from frozen, warm through in a preheated oven at gas mark 4/180°C/350°F for 20 minutes.

Whipped Orange Sauce

serves 4–6

1 I use a double boiler to make this sauce. Pour water in the bottom pan, and heat until almost simmering. If you don't have a double boiler, rest a large bowl over a pan so the bottom of the bowl is about 5 cm/2 inches from the bottom of the pan. Fill the pan with water until just under the base of the bowl.

2 Put the egg yolks into the bowl and whisk to break them up, then add the caster sugar and whisk until pale and foamy.

3 Whisk in the orange juice and Cointreau liqueur, and continue whisking for at least 5 minutes until the sauce has doubled in volume and is foamy. It should just be starting to hold its shape, with the consistency of thick cream.

4 Serve warm or chilled. You can make this sauce 1-2 hours in advance, but it will separate if you make it too far in advance.

2 large egg yolks

25 g/1 oz caster sugar

2 tablespoons orange juice

1 tablespoon Cointreau liqueur

Menu 29

Christmas Menu

Menu
29

Butter-spiced Turkey

Chestnut Stuffing

Crisp Roast Potatoes

Roasted Vegetables

Yorkshire Puddings

Tomato Sauce

Fruity Christmas Pudding

Rum Sauce

Turkey Cooking Times

small (3.5-5 kg/8-11 lb)

start at gas mark 7/220°C/425°F for 30 minutes
turn down to gas mark 3/160°C/325°F for 3 hours
finish at gas mark 6/200°C/400°F for 30 minutes

Total cooking time: 4 hours + leave to stand for 30 minutes

medium (5.5-6.5 kg/12-14 lb)

start at gas mark 7/220°C/425°F for 45 minutes
turn down to gas mark 3/160°C/325°F for 3½ hours
finish at gas mark 6/200°C/400°F for 45 minutes

Total cooking time: 5 hours + leave to stand for 35 minutes

large (6.75-9 kg/15-20 lb)

start at gas mark 7/220°C/425°F for 1 hour
turn down to 3/160°C/325°F for 4½ hours
finish at gas mark 6/200°C/400°F for 45 minutes

Total cooking time: 6¼ hours + leave to stand for 40 minutes

Butter-spiced Turkey

serves 5

I think a fresh, free-range turkey is worth the extra money for the better flavour you get. Many people buy a turkey that is too big, and then get tired of the leftovers. To avoid this, allow 500 g/1 lb per person of oven-ready weight for the main meal only, but buy 750 g/ 1½ lb per person if you do want some leftovers.

1 Beat the cinnamon and mixed spice into the butter until well mixed.

2 Put half the butter mixture into the main body cavity of the turkey, along with the onion and thyme.

3 Smear the rest of the butter over the surface of the turkey, getting as much as possible over the top of the breast.

4 Tie the legs together with string, taking the string around the Parson's nose to make a neat shape, or tuck the ends of the legs through the rear end. You can enlarge this vent yourself, if necessary. The flap of skin at the neck end will fold under to hold any stuffing in (don't stuff too tightly, as the stuffing will expand a little during cooking). You can fasten the skin with a skewer if you think it needs it.

5 Place 1 large, long strip of kitchen foil over your biggest roasting tin, then place another strip across it, to make a large cross. Place the turkey in the centre, then fold the opposite sides of the foil up to make a tent over the turkey. Fold the edges together, but leave plenty of space inside the tent, so any steam can circulate.

6 When you have decided at what time you want to eat, calculate the cooking time required (see chart overleaf for cooking time and temperature), and place the turkey in a preheated oven. You will see that I have added 'resting' time. This is very important: by leaving it to rest, it will carve and taste much better, and it will keep hot for the whole time, if kept in a fairly warm kitchen.

7 Baste the turkey with the buttery juices at least once during the cooking time. During the 'finish' time of the cooking, fold back the foil so the breast browns, and baste again.

8 To check the turkey is cooked through at the end of the cooking time, pierce the thickest part of the thigh and see if the juices run clear. If the juices are slightly pink, put the turkey back in the oven to cook until done.

2 teaspoons ground cinnamon

2 teaspoons ground mixed spice

250 g/8 oz butter, softened

1 × 5.5 kg/5 lb turkey

½ onion (there is no need to peel it)

small bunch of thyme

Note
You could also serve this with Chestnut Croquettes (see page 100).

Chestnut Stuffing

makes enough to stuff a medium-sized turkey

50 g/2 oz bacon, chopped into small pieces

25 g/1 oz butter

100 g/3½ oz breadcrumbs

2 tablespoons chopped parsley

250 g/8 oz chestnut purée (unsweetened)

1 egg, beaten

salt and pepper

1 Fry the bacon until crisp in the butter, then tip the bacon with the buttery juices into a bowl and add the other ingredients.

2 Mix well with a fork, and use to stuff the neck end of the turkey (see step 4 of Butter-spiced Turkey). Alternatively, put the stuffing into an ovenproof dish and level the top with a fork. Bake in a preheated oven at gas mark 6/200°C/400°F for 15 minutes.

Crisp Roast Potatoes

serves 6

If you roast a duck or goose, be sure to save the fat from the roasting tin – it's excellent for roast potatoes. Use whatever old potatoes you can find, but I like Wilja best.

1 tablespoon vegetable oil

1 tablespoon butter

1 kg/2 lbs potatoes, peeled and cut into large chunks

salt

1 Put the oil and butter into a roasting tin, and heat in the oven at gas mark 7/220°C/425°F while you do the next step.

2 Put the potatoes into lightly salted water and bring up to the boil. Simmer for 10 minutes, then drain well. Put the lid on the potatoes and shake the pan three times – you will need to protect your hands with a cloth or oven glove – to rough up the edges of the potatoes.

3 Remove the hot fat from the oven, and add the drained potatoes. Turn the potatoes to coat them in the fat. Put back into the oven, and roast for 15 minutes. Turn the potatoes, then roast for a further 20-30 minutes, until crisp and golden brown.

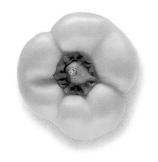

Roasted Vegetables

This makes a good accompaniment for any meat dish, but in case you have any non-meat eaters around your table, I'd suggest serving the same vegetables piled into individual Yorkshire puddings and accompanying this with Tomato Sauce instead of gravy.

2 garlic cloves, crushed

2 tablespoons olive oil

a selection of raw vegetables (about 250 g/8 oz per person), such as parsnip, red onion, courgette, yellow pepper and carrot, peeled and cut into chunks

1 Place the garlic in a roasting tin with the olive oil, and heat together on the hob until the oil starts to sizzle.

2 Add the vegetable chunks, and mix well until they are coated with oil.

3 Roast in a preheated oven at gas mark 6/200°C/400°F for about 30 minutes, turning once halfway through cooking. When the vegetables are crisp and browned at the edges, but still with some bite in the centre, they are cooked.

Note
When preparing the chunks of vegetables to roast, cut the ones that take longer to cook into smaller pieces, for example, carrot would be smaller than courgette.

Yorkshire Puddings

makes 10–12 individual puddings if made in muffin tins, 8 in Yorkshire pudding tins

1 Whisk together the eggs and milk, using either a food processor, blender, or an electric whisk. While still whisking, gradually add the flour and salt. The batter is ready when bubbles start to form on the surface. Leave the batter to stand for ½ hour, then add a tablespoon of cold water, and whisk again.

2 Put a little oil (about 1 dessertspoon, or less) into each muffin or pudding tin, and place in a preheated oven at gas mark 7/220°C/425°F for about 5 minutes. To check if the oil is hot enough, drop a tiny amount of batter into one of the indentations. If it sizzles, it's ready.

3 Pour the batter into the indentations, until about one-third full, and place back in the oven for 15-20 minutes, until the puddings are risen and golden brown.

2 medium eggs

300 ml/½ pint milk

125 g/4 oz white plain flour

¼ teaspoon salt

vegetable oil, for greasing

Tomato Sauce

serves 4

1 Heat the oil in a saucepan, and gently fry the onion and garlic until the onion has softened, but not browned.

2 Add the tomatoes, herbs and tomato purée, and season well. Simmer together for about 10 minutes, until slightly thickened. You can serve the sauce like this if you like it chunky, or purée it until smooth in a blender or food processor, and re-heat.

2 tablespoons olive oil

1-2 garlic cloves, crushed

½ large onion, chopped

425 g/14 oz tinned chopped tomatoes

2 teaspoons dried mixed herbs or 1 tablespoon freshly chopped basil or oregano

1 tablespoon tomato purée

salt and pepper

Fruity Christmas Pudding

serves 6

75 g/3 oz wholemeal or white plain flour

½ teaspoon ground cinnamon

½ teaspoon ground nutmeg

1 teaspoon ground mixed spice

a pinch of salt

25 g/1 oz wholemeal breadcrumbs

75 g/3 oz vegetarian suet

75 g/3 oz soft dark brown sugar

100 g/3½ oz glacé cherries

100 g/3½ oz sultanas

100 g/3½ oz raisins

100 g/3½ oz dried apricots, finely chopped

50 g/2 oz ground almonds

1 small or ½ large cooking apple, peeled and grated

2 eggs, beaten

2 tablespoons brandy

2 tablespoons black treacle, warmed

grated zest and juice of 1 small orange

a little milk

butter, for greasing

Most traditional Christmas puddings need to be made well in advance, and then need steaming for hours. This doesn't always fit in with today's modern lifestyles, so although this looks and tastes like the old-fashioned steamed puddings, it is actually made only the day before – and is cooked in the microwave! Trust me – it will taste delicious. You'll see that I've used apricots, which I think are moister and tastier than currants.

1 Put the flour, cinnamon, nutmeg, mixed spice, a pinch of salt and the breadcrumbs into a large mixing bowl and mix together.

2 Add the suet, sugar, glacé cherries, sultanas, raisins, apricots, almonds and apple, and mix again.

3 Add the eggs, brandy, black treacle and orange zest and juice and mix well. When all the ingredients are well mixed, you need to test the consistency. You are aiming for a soft, dropping consistency, which means that if you lift up some of the mixture on a wooden spoon, it drops back into the bowl without having to shake the spoon. Add a little milk if the mixture seems too stiff.

4 Cover the bowl, and place in a cool larder or in the fridge. Leave overnight for the flavours to develop and mingle.

5 The next day, stir the mixture then spoon it into a greased 1.2 litre/2 pint pudding basin. Cover with clingfilm, and then pierce all over the film with a skewer.

6 Cook in a microwave on high for 10 minutes, then leave to stand for a further 10 minutes before turning out onto a serving plate.

Rum Sauce

makes 900 ml/1½ pints

This all-in-one method works well, but you must keep stirring all the time. I find it easiest if I use a small whisk.

1 Pour the milk into a small pan, add the butter and stir over a low heat until melted.

2 Tip in the flour, all at once, and immediately start whisking. The sauce will thicken as it comes up to the boil, and as soon as it starts to bubble, turn the heat down and continue to whisk for 2-3 minutes.

3 Remove from the heat, and stir in the sugar until dissolved. Finally add the rum and cream and stir well.

4 To keep the sauce warm until needed, cover with clingfilm. This will also stop a skin from forming.

600 ml/1 pint milk

75 g/3 oz butter, chopped into small pieces

75 g/3 oz white plain flour

75 g/3 oz caster sugar

4 tablespoons dark rum

1 small carton (approximately 150 ml/¼ pint) single cream

Menu
30

Vegetarian
Christmas Menu

Menu
30

Triple Mushroom Pâté en Croûte

Yorkshire Sauce

Cranberry and Chestnut Bombe

Triple Mushroom Pâté en Croûte

serves 6

This makes an unusual, but still festive, meal for Christmas, and is designed to please those who like something a bit different, as well as for vegetarians. Serve with a selection of your favourite winter vegetables, or one of the vegetable recipes featured in the other Christmas menus.

1 Start by making the pâté. Pour the boiling water over the dried mushrooms, and leave to soak for at least 1 hour, longer if possible. Drain, and rinse under a tap, to get rid of any little pieces of grit.

2 Melt the butter in a large pan and gently fry the onion for 5 minutes, until it starts to turn transparent.

3 Add the button or cup mushrooms to the onion mixture, mix, and cook gently for a further 5 minutes.

4 Use a pair of scissors to snip the soaked mushrooms into the pan, then add the wine. Bring up to the boil and simmer without a lid for about 1 hour, until the mixture thickens and becomes almost dry. You will need to stir it from time to time and keep an eye on it, stirring more towards the end.

5 Stir in the mushroom ketchup and season well with salt and pepper. Set aside the mushroom pâté to cool a little, while you make the rest of the dish.

6 In a small frying pan, melt the butter and add the garlic and mushrooms. Cook for 2-3 minutes until the mushrooms start to soften.

7 On a well-floured surface, roll out the puff pastry to make a rectangle about 40 × 30 cm/16 × 12 inches. Place the pastry rectangle on a large piece of foil, which will help to lift it when filled.

8 Spoon the mushroom pâté lengthways down the middle third of the pastry, leaving a space around the edge of the pastry. Spread the fried mushroom mixture over the top of this.

9 Fold the ends of the pastry over to hold the pâté in place, and brush the long sides of the pastry with water. Bring the sides together to meet in the centre, squeezing them to hold together and form a ridge, rather like a Cornish pasty.

10 Brush generously with beaten egg all over the surface. Bake in a preheated oven at gas mark 6/200°C/400°F for 20-30 minutes, until the pastry is crisp and golden brown, all over.

11 Serve cut into 6 thick slices. You may wish to discard the ends, which will be mostly pastry, but there will still be plenty for 6 good servings.

25 g/1 oz butter

1 garlic clove, crushed

40 g /1½ oz fresh mushrooms (preferably oyster or shitaake, but you could use button), sliced

flour, for dusting

375 g/12 oz puff pastry

a little beaten egg, to glaze

FOR THE MUSHROOM PÂTÉ:

300 ml/½ pint boiling water

15 g/½ oz dried mixed mushrooms (e.g. porcini, ceps and woodland fungi)

50 g/2 oz butter

125 g/4 oz onion, chopped

500 g/1 lb button or cup mushrooms, finely chopped

450 ml/¾ pint red wine

2 teaspoons mushroom ketchup

salt and pepper

Yorkshire Sauce

makes about 450 ml/¾ pint

This was originally served with York ham at Christmas time, but is equally good with other dishes. I have given two versions, a thick version and a thin one, so you can please yourself how you serve it. Some recipes say to thicken the sauce using cornflour, but this makes the sauce opaque. I find arrowroot gives a nicer, glossy finish.

grated zest and juice of 2 oranges

200 ml/7 fl oz port

¼ teaspoon ground cinnamon

2 tablespoons redcurrant jelly

2 teaspoons arrowroot (optional)

2 tablespoons water (optional)

1 Mix the orange zest with the port and leave to infuse, for 1 hour, or longer if possible.

2 Add all the other ingredients except for the arrowroot (if using), and heat through in a pan, stirring until the redcurrant jelly has melted. If you like a thin sauce, this is now ready to serve.

3 For a thick sauce, mix the arrowroot to a smooth paste with the water. Add to the sauce in the pan and bring to a simmer, stirring gently. The sauce will clear and thicken as it starts to simmer, and at this point it will only need to cook for a further 30 seconds. Any longer and you will boil off all the alcohol from the port.

Cranberry and Chestnut Bombe

serves 6

I started to make this recipe because a friend said that most puddings at Christmas time have dried fruit in them, which she doesn't like. This seems to get in some of the traditional flavours without the currants and sultanas, and the mixture of rum, cranberries and chestnuts works well.

Dried cranberries are available before Christmas in most supermarkets, but you could use fresh or frozen ones, in which case you would need to double the quantity, as the flavour has not been concentrated by drying. Thaw frozen cranberries before using.

1 Put the rum and cranberries into a small saucepan and heat gently until almost boiling, then remove from the heat and leave to cool, for at least 30 minutes.

2 Line a 2.25 litre/4 pint pudding bowl or glass mixing bowl with clingfilm. Place in the fridge to chill.

3 Meanwhile, whisk the egg yolks and caster sugar together until pale and thick. Add the vanilla extract and chestnut purée and whisk until there are no lumps.

4 Gently stir in the rum and cranberry mixture, then add the chopped marrons glacés. Place in the fridge to keep cool while you get on with the rest of the recipe.

5 Whip the double cream until it is thick and floppy and is just holding its shape, then fold it into the chestnut mixture.

6 In a clean bowl, whisk the egg whites until stiff, then fold into the chestnut mixture. Pour the mixture into the lined bowl, and place in a freezer overnight.

7 When you are ready to serve the bombe, use the clingfilm to help you turn it out onto a serving dish. If you wish, decorate with whirls of whipped cream topped with marrons glacés, dried cranberries and a dredging of icing sugar.

80 ml/3 fl oz dark rum

75 g/3 oz dried cranberries

4 eggs, separated

75 g/3 oz caster sugar

1 teaspoon vanilla extract

1 tin (approximately 425 g/14 oz) unsweetened chestnut purée

125 g/4 oz marrons glacés, chopped roughly

400 ml/14 fl oz double cream

TO DECORATE (OPTIONAL):

whipped cream

marrons glacés

dried cranberries

icing sugar, to dredge

Recipe Index

A

B

C

D

E

F

G

H